Architecting the Web

A Full Stack Developer's Guide to Build Scalable Apps

Publisher
COPAL Publishing Group
E-143, Lajpat Nagar, Sahibabad,
Distt. Ghaziabad, UP – 201005, India
https://copalpublishing.com

First Published 2025

ISBN: 978-81-987543-56

Printed and bound by D K Fine Art Press, New Delhi

Architecting the Web

A Full Stack Developer's Guide to Build Scalable Apps

Dr. Arulkumar Varatharajan

Dr. Lokeshkumar Ramasamy

COPAL PUBLISHING GROUP

Inspiring for a better future through publishing

Preface

In order to thrive in today's ever-changing digital landscape, developers must become experts in creating web applications that are both scalable and robust. If you're a full-stack developer or just starting out and want to learn how to build apps that can handle increasing complexity, *Architecting the Web* is a must-read.

The book mainly aims to bridge the gap between basic ideas and current practices. It delves into the many aspects of full-stack development, including database management, server-side architecture, user interface design, and front-end development. Scalability, maintainability, and performance optimization are some of the key ideas that readers will learn about, and they will also learn about the tools and techniques that are necessary to put these ideas into practice.

Architecting the Web rests on three main points: Developer collaboration, technological ecosystems, and system design. Building resilient, scalable systems that can adapt to users' changing needs is a central theme throughout the book. It delves into the ecosystems of tech, frameworks, and tools that make development productive and efficient. Finally, it promotes best practices for cooperation in current development environments and highlights the significance of collaborative workflows.

This book will teach you the basics of building scalable and sustainable web apps, whether you're just starting out as a developer or are an experienced pro. Inspiring, educating, and empowering you to push web development to its limits is the goal of each chapter.

Contents

1 Introduction to Advanced Web Development

1.1 Overview of Modern Web Technologies

Internet-connected devices enable users to access the international information network known as the Web or World Wide Web (WWW). End-users receive the web service through the Internet. The Internet developed as a technology framework much prior to World Wide Web technologies. Several professionals refer to the Internet through the name "network of networks." People in the current generation actively use internet services from the World Wide Web without recognizing how these services work under the surface. New technological advancements enable complete abstraction of the Internet together with the Web from their fundamental technical processes. The unit introduces fundamental Internet knowledge for web application developers while presenting essential information about Internet and web components.

1.2 Evolution of Web Development: From HTML to Full-Stack Applications

Web development has experienced a major transformation because developers built applications that created dynamic, interactive web pages. Starting from their simple origins, websites presented static information that users could only browse through based on their selection choices. Web content began generating dynamically when CGI (Common Gateway Interface) scripts were brought into use for the production of dynamic content.

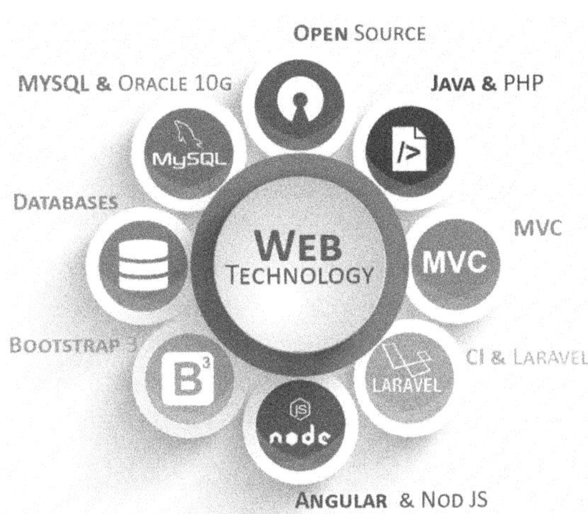

Figure 1.1 Overview of modern web technologies

The combination of AJAX (Asynchronous JavaScript and XML) technology during the late 1990s through early 2000s created more compelling web applications by enabling background server and web page data communication that produced asynchronous content. The development framework duo Ruby on Rails and Django arrived in the hands of web developers to enhance application speed and streamline workflow operations.

Web development experienced significant advancement through the integration of HTML5, CSS3, and ECMAScript 6 (ES6) version of JavaScript. These technological advancements in web applications produced improved user-friendly interfaces that used animations as well as enhanced application logic that was easier for users.

The success of contemporary web applications like Gmail and Google Docs serves as evidence that enables understanding of these technological progressions. The AJAX-based interface of Gmail proved to experts that web applications could replicate desktop functionality effectively. The online collaboration feature of Google Docs competed directly with traditional office suites by enabling users to work together simultaneously. This part explores these various milestones with a focus on their role in web development evolution as well as their establishment for present-day and upcoming technological achievements.

1.2.1 Rise of Frameworks and Libraries

Web application development underwent substantial transformation because of framework and library creation. The web application development industry gained powerful development tools through AngularJS, which Google released in 2010, along with React from Facebook in 2013. The combination of different frameworks with Vue.js allowed developers to create applications using structured development methods that shortened development time along with decreased complexity.

1.2.2 Advancements in Web Standards

Web application functionality has significantly improved through the standardization process for web development. Both HTML5 and CSS3 introduced semantic elements and APIs for application operation enhancement and added transitions along with animations with responsive design features enabled from CSS3. ES6 introduced coding improvements as well as browser compatibility benefits using new syntax and features. Sophisticated interactive web applications became possible through the innovations that ensure their fluid operation between different devices and platforms.

1.2.3 The Impact of Mobile Development

The evolution of web standards has molded the operational possibilities of web applications into their current state. Semantic elements and application programming interfaces (APIs) came with HTML5 to enhance functionality along with the styling features from CSS3 that included transitions and animations and responsive design using the flexbox. The introduction of ES6 provided JavaScript with fresh syntax together with new features that established improved coding methods alongside better browser compatibility. Web applications gained enhanced functionality due to developments that let developers create complicated interactive applications that operated without issues across various devices and platforms.

1.3 Current State of Web Application Development

1.3.1 Modern Development Technologies and Frameworks

At present the market for web application development provides multiple technological frameworks that form its current landscape. The combination of Vue.js with React and Angular dominates frontend development through the unique advantages that provide developers with excellent performance and flexibility. With its server-side scripting function, Node.js provides developers the capability to perform complete stack development utilizing JavaScript.

1.3.2 APIs and Microservices Architecture

Web applications undertake transformative changes after implementing both application programming interfaces and microservices architecture. Through this construction methodology, the developer can maintain separate units of development for applications, which helps them work independently on particular sections of application development. The design methodology allows organizations to preserve automated deployment techniques that speed up development while improving operational efficiency.

1.3.3 Emphasis on User Experience and Performance

Modern web development centers its efforts on UX and application performance delivery. PWAs function like applications by operating offline while delivering immediate load times to users. Speed optimization of web applications depends on two essential components, which are performance optimization techniques, including code splitting and asset delivery optimization.

1.3.4 Security Considerations

Web applications have developed increasing complexity, which has made security the top priority for today's development world. Web development practices of today integrate security features at their start by using HTTPS and implementing Content Security Policy (CSP) as well as cross-origin resource sharing (CORS) policies.

1.3.5 Detailed Methodology

A research study consisting of 100 development teams selected five members per team to participate in the study. Criteria for selection included:

• At least two programming languages from the spectrum of web development must be mastered by the developer.

• Frontend and backend development experience forms a necessary requirement for applicants.

• A portfolio of completed web projects.

1.3.6 Technologies Used

(i) Control Group (Traditional Stack)

HTML5, CSS3, JavaScript (ES6), jQuery

Server-side scripting requires PHP 7 or Python 3, while database requirements include MySQL or PostgreSQL, and deployment uses Apache or Nginx as the web server.

(ii) Experimental Group (Modern Technologies)

The present-day development world focuses on security as the main priority because web applications have grown increasingly complex. Modern web development practices begin with built-in security measures that use HTTPS plus Content Security Policy together with cross-origin resource sharing policy implementations. A web application stays shielded from XSS (Cross-

Site Scripting) and CSRF (Cross-Site Request Forgery) attacks if security best practices maintain constant updates while vulnerability scanning takes place.

1.3.7 Tools and Platforms

All project teams received Integrated Development Environment (IDE) Visual Studio Code and Version Control system Git with GitHub, as well as Testing Instruments Jest for JavaScript testing along with PyTest for Python and PHPUnit for PHP as their resources.

Visual Studio Code IDE with Git through GitHub and the testing tools Jest for JavaScript and PyTest for Python and PHPUnit for PHP made up the shared resources for all project teams.

(i) Development Time

The teams tracked their whole development cycle duration using built-in time-tracking software inside the IDE.

(ii) Performance Metrics

The teams deployed every project through Lighthouse and WebPageTest, which automatically tracked important performance results. The metrics focused on were:

(a) The site requires a specific amount of time to display its first byte to the user. Time to Interactive represents the complete interactivity state of the website.

(b) The screen display receives the initial text or image items through First Contentful Paint after a specified amount of time.

(iii) User Satisfaction

The user satisfaction evaluation depended upon surveys distributed to random users who accessed the team-developed applications. NPS served as the chosen evaluation method for user satisfaction within the survey design.

Web application development experiences fundamental changes because of these factors.

1.3.8 Progressive Web Apps (PWAs)

The development of web applications through Progressive Web Apps provides a transformational method that generates fast, reliable, interactive online interfaces. Modern web capabilities enable PWAs to provide application-like experiences to users so they face diminishing differences between web content and applications. PWAs offer two important features: offline operation and automatic background updates and push notifications that deliver improved user experiences.

Major brands, together with leading platforms, now embrace PWAs because these digital services boost visitor retention and sales numbers, thus proving their central role in upcoming web technology.

1.3.9 Serverless Architecture

Serverless computing changes the building process of applications while managing deployment through a more efficient and cost-effective web development approach. Software developers no longer need to manage infrastructure when they abstract the server layer because they can then focus exclusively on code creation.

These new development systems use event-based designs that automate scalability according to demand needs, thus enhancing operational efficiency and cost reduction and improving overall system performance. Web development implements serverless architectures through cloud service expansion that now includes AWS Lambda, Azure Functions, and Google Cloud Functions.

1.3.10 Artificial Intelligence and Machine Learning

The development process for websites now requires artificial intelligence (AI) and machine learning (ML) because they speed up regular workflows and strengthen human-machine interactions. Web development applications benefit from AI and ML solutions because they reinforce user participation as well as enable novel product development.

1.3.11 Internet of Things (IoT) Integration

Current web development is being stretched to its limits by merging IoT devices with web-based systems. Users can achieve seamless digital-physical interface management through web interfaces built from the combination of IoT devices and web applications. User experience improvements will depend on advanced interaction possibilities brought by incorporating IoT devices into web applications as they become increasingly abundant on the market.

1.4 Development Environments and Tools

Software developers need development tools and environments that combine both hardware elements and software applications to build code and conduct testing and debugging before application release. Coding environments with necessary technical tools enable developers to achieve efficient management and development of software code.

1.4.1 What Is a Development Environment?

A development environment consists of procedural tools that aid developers in program testing and debugging applications as well as websites. Softer development partners use the term DSP for referring to the three standard server types. They are:

(i) The development server functions as the initial stage that lets developers check application code sections and confirm their operational success. After developers finish a series of evaluation and testing exams, the new code passes the tests successfully; the following phase begins.

(ii) The staging server requires developers to build an environment that simulates the end product through its framework. Developers test the application's integrity and reliability on the staging environment before deploying it to the production server after gaining approval.

(iii) The production server serves as the final part of the environment. The developers deploy the application to the server after confirming its success status.

1.4.2 What Is an Integrated Development Environment?

The integrated development environment (IDE) functions as a software program that provides programming developers with efficient tools to build software code. The combination of software editing with building, testing, and packaging tools in a single application platform enhances development speed while increasing developer effectiveness. Software developers require IDEs for the same essential purpose as writers use text editors and accountants use spreadsheets.

IDEs provide development advantages that surpass textual code-authoring since they consolidate developer tools into a unified environment. Through these comprehensive development platforms, programmers achieve process optimization through the centralization of programming tools. The acceleration of new application development becomes possible through this approach while the manual combination and setup of different tools become obsolete. There exist numerous appealing motives that push developers toward using IDEs.

(i) Code Editing Automation

The programming language rules that IDEs understand allow them to provide intelligent automation features that streamline coding together with editing operations. IDEs make code more readable through automatic formatting, which makes keywords bold as they apply different font colors to programming elements. The visual signals simply reveal possible syntax mistakes in real-time.

Intelligent Code Completion

IDEs typically present code completion recommendations during user typing, which quickens the coding work.

IDEs enable developers to perform code refactoring, which enhances code efficiency alongside readability by maintaining original core functionalities. The system supports maintainable code and enhances teamwork projects.

1.4.3 What Are Development Tools?

Program software tools exist for software developers to make other applications ready for distribution and debugging through editing and maintenance features. Such tools receive alternative names as software programming tools. Several types of tools used in software development include linkers together with code editors and GUI designers as well as performance analysis tools and assemblers and compilers.

Software development tools prove necessary in development processes because they enable programmers to achieve various essential goals.

(1) These tools help software development to become more productive when applied to project work.

(2) The development tools let developers keep project workflow under control through simple maintenance procedures.

(3) Systems developed by developers benefit from quality code implementations due to software platforms and add-ons and developer tools that increase coding efficiency.

(4) Mobile application development tools aid developers to construct mobile applications and their designs as well as perform testing before releasing them across various operating systems and devices.

(5) Through the Chrome Developer Tools, developers gain entry to the hidden workings of web browsers together with web applications.

There are many software development tools available in the market today. Some of the best software development tools include:

• Embold operates as a software analytics platform to assist developers in addressing issues that arise before system release.

• Linx functions as a tool that relies on low-code programming to automate backend development of web services and applications.

Table 1.1 Development tools: Advantage and disadvantage

Advantage	Disadvantage
Efficiency: Development tools can greatly increase the efficiency of software development by automating repetitive tasks.	**Learning Curve:** Each tool has its own features and usage, so developers need to spend time learning how to use them effectively.
Quality Control: Tools like debuggers and compilers help maintain high standards of code quality	**Dependency:** Over-reliance on tools can lead to a lack of fundamental programming skills.
Collaboration: Many development tools facilitate collaboration among team members, making it easier to work on large projects.	**Limitations:** Every tool has its limitations and may not be suitable for every projector team.
Flexibility: Some development methodologies allow for changes at any stage of the project without delaying the completion date.	**Cost:** Some advanced development tools are expensive, which might be a barrier for small teams or individual developers.

• Zoho Creator presents a platform that enables users to create robust enterprise software applications at 10 times faster speeds.

• ClickUp serves as a project management tool that includes superior bug tracking functions alongside sprint management, core automation, and collaborative features.

• GitHub exists as a cloud development platform that enables developers to use version control through its services.

• The Azure platform delivers cloud computing solutions as well as many services to help users construct, execute, and administer applications.

Development tools, like any other tools, have their pros and cons. Here are some of them:

Development tools and environments are integral to modern software development, providing the necessary infrastructure, automation, and efficiency that developers rely on to create high-quality software. Integrated Development Environments (IDEs) streamline the coding process, while various other development tools enhance productivity, code quality, and collaboration. However, developers should strike a balance between tool usage and fundamental programming skills to avoid over-dependency and carefully consider the suitability and cost of tools for their specific projects and teams.

1.5 Key Concepts in Web Application Architecture

The following part will introduce several web-related definitions that may already be familiar to readers for learning about the World Wide Web.

1.5.1 Hypertext, Hyperlink, Uniform Resource Locator (URL)

The text on computer displays together with its linking references constitutes hypertext. Hypertext is text with hyperlinks. Hypertext describes various types of presentation content, such as text and tables, along with images that contain hyperlinks between them. The fundamental structure of the World Wide Web depends on hypertext, which uses Hypertext Markup Language (HTML) as its standard page-writing language.

Links represent data references in any system. A hyperlink points to a whole document or to a specific element within a document. Users can activate hyperlinks through mouse clicks or sequences of keys or by using the screen.

A Uniform Resource Locator (URL) stands as a unique sequence of characters that functions as an internet resource reference. The top section of most web browsers displays the web page URL through an address bar. The uniform resource locator (URL) enables users to access web pages through http://www.google.co.in and also serves as a protocol for file transfer (ftp:), email (mailto:), and telephone numbers (tel:).

1.5.2 Hypertext Transfer Protocol (HTTP)

HTTP functions as an application protocol that serves as the protocol for exchanging and transferring hypertext. Data communication for the World Wide Web operates on the basis of HTTP. A series of Requests for Comments (RFCs) appeared from the Internet Engineering Task Force (IETF) along with the World Wide Web Consortium (W3C) for standards development of HTTP. RFC 2616 (on June 1999) defined HTTP/1.1, which remains in widespread use today.

The TCP/IP Suite framework contains this stateless application layer protocol named HTTP. Back-to-back client-server transactions through the network form a session under HTTP. An HTTP client begins a session by connecting through Transmission Control Protocol (TCP) to a port of the server where 80 is the default but others exist. The port listener function of the HTTP server maintains readiness to receive data from client request messages until a message arrives from clients. After the server receives the request, it responds with both a status line that contains "HTTP/1.1 200 OK" and its message body. The main message content consists of the requested resource, or it returns alternative content like error information. With HTTP, servers allow standardized computer communication through the Internet along with other devices. The HTTP specification defines the procedures for client requests and server responses regarding data transmission construction and receipt.

1.5.3 Hypertext Transfer Protocol Secure (HTTPS)

Through Hypertext Transfer Protocol Secure (HTTPS), users can access or send their Internet information in a highly secure way. There exists a security encryption method for all data moving through HTTPS, which protects the information when transmitted across the Internet. The data encryption process during HTTPS transmission leads to reduced speed compared to the standard HTTP protocol but ensures secure data transfer; therefore, HTTPS is specifically used for protected transfers. Login pages, along with those that include sensitive information such as online bank accounts, require HTTPS encryption. HTTPS uses port 443.

1.5.4 Domain Name System (DNS)

DNS functions as a service that translates complete domain names into corresponding IP addresses while converting them into each other. Users can remember domain names better through "www.kkhsou.in" rather than IP addresses such as "182.50.130.66." Moreover, IP addresses may change. It would become harder to maintain memorization of numbers if we used them instead of domain names.

A nameserver functions as a DNS server to perform network-based hostname-to-IP address association services. The implementation of DNS requires one or multiple servers that function as domain authorities for specific domains. The client host establishes port 53 connections with nameservers for information requests. The nameserver starts by processing the requested name. It first checks its local storage to respond authoritatively or retrieve cached records from past queries, but if unsuccessful, it will query root nameservers to obtain the nameservers that control the requested name and then request the name from those servers.

1.5.5 TCP/IP: The Protocol of the Internet

The Internet protocol suite functions as both a networking model and a standard protocol collection that operates the Internet. TCP/IP represents the common industry terminology because Transmission Control Protocol (TCP) and Internet Protocol (IP) originally stood as the crucial protocols within this standard. The networking model receives sporadic references as the DoD (Department of Defense) model because DARPA funded its development as an agency within the United States Department of Defense.

The TCP/IP communication system enables end-to-end data delivery by determining formatting standards along with transmission protocols, routing methods, and destination delivery techniques. Thorough functionality relates to four groups of abstractions. The Link Layer serves as the fundamental layer, followed by the Internet Layer, which exists above it; then the Transport Layer rests above the Internet Layer, while the highest layer is the Application Layer.

The model arranges functionalities into four abstraction layers that start from the lower Link Layer and end with the upper Application Layer, which provides support services for users. The Internet Engineering Task Force (IETF) protects both the TCP/IP model together with its related protocols.

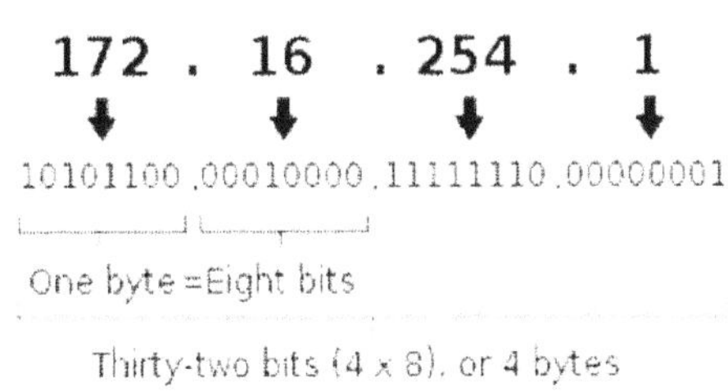

Figure 1.1 An IPV4 address (dotted-decimal notation)

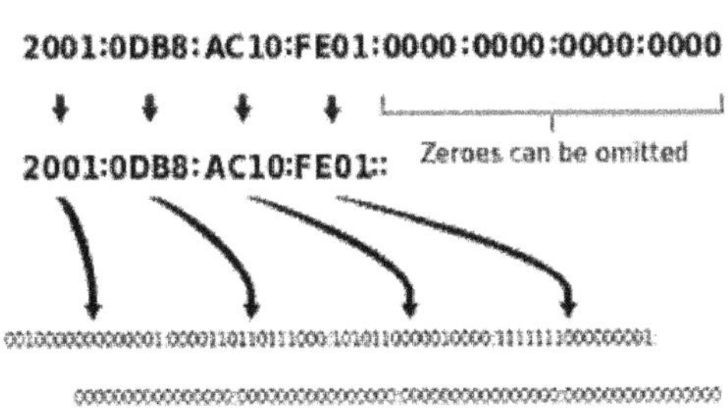

Figure 1.2 An IPV6 address (In hexadecimal)

1.5.6 Internet Protocol (IP) and the Concept of IP Addresses

Every device that operates in a computer network employing Internet Protocol requires a numerical code known as an Internet Protocol address, which binds to a laptop, desktop, server, printer, Wi-Fi router, etc., and all their counterparts. Two diverse versions control Internet Protocol networks today, with IPv4 employing 32-bit addressing and IPv6 employing 128-bit addressing. The development of IPv6 in 1995 occurred because the Internet experienced significant expansion, which led to the anticipated exhaustion of IPv4 address availability.

The storage of binary IP addresses occurs as text files that display human-readable notations using IPv4 addresses in dotted decimal format 192.168.1.1 or the IPv6 format fda8:06c3:ce53:a890:0000:0000:0000:0001.

The logical parts of IP network systems use a subnet mask for their segmentation process. One can achieve subnetting through network partitioning into multiple separate networks. During IP address segmentation, the subnet mask establishes which part of an IP address becomes the network region and the host segment. The number of bits used to identify network and host addresses within an IP address gets determined by subnet masks through their specifications.

Each computer device inside a network needs to use a distinct and unique IP address to establish successful interactions through networking devices.

The Internet Assigned Numbers Authority (IANA) oversees global IP address space distribution while giving five regional Internet registries (RIRs) authority through their allocations to local Internet registries (Internet service providers) and additional entities.

1.5.7 Internet Service Provider (ISP), Autonomous System (AS)

The Internet Service Provider functions as the entry point to the Internet alongside providing multiple non-exclusive services such as domain name registration, email services, dial-up connection, and leased line hosting.

An autonomous system acts as a connected network group that includes multiple IP prefixes (network prefixes) that one or more network operators run using a single unified routing policy. Every Internet Service Provider needs an officially registered Autonomous System Number to operate. The BGP routing system needs unique AS numbers assigned to each autonomous system. AS numbers play a crucial role since they provide distinct identification for all Internet networks.

1.5.8 Web Browser and Web Server

The web server software functions as a content delivery system that manages Internet-based website accessibility. Modern web server software platforms such as Apache, Microsoft IIS, Nginx, and Google GWS exist in various product markets.

Through web servers, users can access World Wide Web resources using browsers that retrieve and present the information. Web pages, images, and videos, along with other content pieces, are examples of information resources that obtain their identification through Uniform Resource Identifiers (URIs/URLs). Through resource web links, users can browse their browser to connected resources without difficulty. Among web browser applications, you can find Google Chrome, Mozilla Firefox, Internet Explorer, Opera, and Safari.

2 HTML: The Foundation of Web Development

2.1 Advanced HTML: Beyond the Basics

2.1.1 Introduction to Advanced HTML Concepts

The central requirement for web development exists in Hypertext Mark-up Language, which is commonly known as HTML. The basic elements people perceive in HTML make up only part of the technology, while advanced HTML explores capabilities for creating interactive, dynamic, and flexible web designs. Several complex HTML techniques, when mastered, enhance both website functionality and user interaction during site navigation. A developer must learn to apply meaningful HTML elements with effective document organization while adding multimedia components while enhancing website speed and execution. Healthy web development depends on all three technologies to build websites that respond to users' screen dimensions.

2.1.2 Semantic HTML: The Power of Meaningful Markup

Semantic HTML allows developers to add elements that directly show the structural meaning of their content. All search engines, together with screen readers, benefit from using HTML elements such as <header>, <footer>, <article>, and <section> which establish clearer document structure. Semantic HTML works as an accessibility tool that enhances SEO by establishing distinct sections of content on web pages. Web developers who include semantic components make their pages accessible to human understanding and search engine processing, thus benefiting the modern search-and-access demands of the web.

2.1.3 Advanced Forms: Beyond Simple Inputs

Web applications need HTML form features to receive information from their users. HTML provides multiple developed form elements that go well past the straightforward input field. The form creation process is improved by HTML elements, which include <textarea>, <select> and <datalist>. The HTML5 form attributes pattern, together with placeholder and required, enables real-time input validation while providing user-friendly input instructions. Advanced form interaction is possible through JavaScript for custom control integration, which enables features like dynamic field validity testing and real-time suggestion capabilities. A form designed effectively will enhance user experience while achieving effective data collection.

2.1.4 Media Integration: Embedding Rich Content

Web experiences of today need the fundamental inclusion of multimedia elements, which include images, audio, and video. HTML contains multiple tags to embed multimedia content through <img> and <audio> and <video>. The embedded media tags provide developers with a way to insert various media files straight into the page while omitting outside plugin dependencies. The advanced implementation of HTML includes using autoplay along with loop and control attributes to control media presentation and combining the source element inside video and audio tags to deliver multiple format options for compatibility. Media queries provide developers with a way to confirm that online media elements expand appropriately based on the screen dimensions of different devices.

2.1.5 The Role of Custom Data Attributes

HTML5 introduced the concept of custom data attributes, represented by the data-* attribute. These attributes allow developers to store custom data within an HTML element without affecting its presentation or behavior. This is particularly useful for integrating JavaScript and other programming languages, as data attributes can be accessed and manipulated dynamically. For example, a <div data-user-id="12345"> could be used to store a unique user identifier, which can then be accessed by JavaScript for further functionality, such as making an AJAX request. This capability helps keep HTML clean and organized while offering flexibility for developers.

2.1.6 Accessible Web Design with ARIA

Users with any disability can experience web content accessibility because Web Content Accessibility Guidelines (WCAG) have now become an industry standard. The HTML programming language helps assistive technologies with additional information through its ARIA (Accessible Rich Internet Applications) roles and attributes. ARIA attributes allow developers to enhance accessibility through responsive web content by assigning roles that include button, navigation, and dialog to select HTML elements. The preferred method for accessibility is semantic HTML, but ARIA becomes essential in cases where semantics are inadequate because it enables interactive elements to be accessible to all users.

2.1.7 Advanced CSS Integration within HTML

The content of the webpage gets structured through HTML while CSS controls how content presents itself on the page. The execution of advanced HTML development includes rare CSS integration techniques that combine external stylesheets with internal stylesheet references and inline CSS constraints. The <link> element allows developers to manage website appearances through external CSS files that control whole-site appearance in a single file. The combination of CSS with HTML produces visual elements that stay properly displayed on any device screen.

2.1.8 Embedding JavaScript for Interactivity

The most compelling feature of contemporary HTML involves its effortless combination with the JavaScript programming language. HTML documents accept JavaScript, which developers can place directly inside the code using <script> tags or by linking external files. The dynamic user experience is enhanced through JavaScript because developers can directly control HTML elements and run form validations, plus enable asynchronous loading functions and animate elements. The ability to work with the DOM using JavaScript functions becomes essential for high-level HTML development. The user experience becomes more responsive through JavaScript because developers can create, modify, or delete HTML elements instantly in real-time.

2.1.9 Microdata and Structured Data for SEO

HTML5 includes Microdata as a specification that enables developers to place structured data elements inside HTML content. Search engines gain better search results because a standardized annotation system is available through this framework. HTML5 uses elements that incorporate <span itemscope itemprop="name"> to specify and identify data. The annotation of standardized data through microdata serves eCommerce websites specifically by enabling search engines to recognize product specifications, including costs, feedback ratings, and inventory details. The implementation of microdata improves website exposure in search engines to increase the chance of achieving better search query rankings.

2.1.10 Performance Optimization: HTML Best Practices

Advanced HTML development has made performance optimization a critical priority because of progressively complex websites. Web pages become more efficient through lazy loading because this technique postpones image and resource loading until the specific moment of utilization. Users with disabled JavaScript can still access essential information through the <noscript> tag that accompanies content that requires JavaScript processing. The optimization process includes removing unneeded code while compressing different files and reducing the number of HTTP requests. A combination of these approaches generates quick user experiences together with better SEO positions.

2.1.11 Responsive Web Design with HTML and CSS

Advanced HTML development requires the <meta> tag with the viewport attribute to enable responsive design effectiveness. The entity of <meta> the viewport attribute works in consonance with CSS media queries to make page layout adjustments as devices change their width, height, or orientation. A unified optimal user experience for desktops, tablets, and smartphones can be achieved through developer utilizations of fluid grids and flexible images along with content scaling methods.

2.1.12 Evolving with the Web

HTML evolves through new versions to offer developers more features, which enable the creation of progressively advanced interactive websites. To maintain leadership in web development, professionals must learn complex HTML practices. The modern web development landscape will depend on the perfectly combined use of HTML with other technologies to develop dynamic, user-focused solutions.

2.2 Semantic Markup and Accessibility Standards

Using markup based on HTML elements allows developers to identify webpage content with precision. Web elements depict content information precisely to developers and simultaneously boost SEO ranking and make websites accessible for users with disabilities. Digital content becomes more usable for people with disabilities through the implementation of accessibility standards, particularly the Web Content Accessibility Guidelines (WCAG).

2.2.1 The Importance of Semantic HTML in Modern Web Development

The HTML tags used in semantic HTML represent and describe the semantic meaning of all contained content. Page structure becomes clear through HTML elements that include <header>, <footer>, <article> and <section> to describe particular webpage sections. The page structure improves browser efficiency in content presentation as well as enabling search engines to create accurate page indexes simultaneously. The semantic coding structure improves website accessibility through its capacity to give meaning and understanding to screen readers and assistive technologies. The screen reader interprets the <header> tag as a navigation area, thus assisting visually impaired users to understand how the page is organized. Through semantic tag implementation, developers make their websites accessible to users and machines at the same time.

2.2.2 Understanding ARIA (Accessible Rich Internet Applications)

The standard foundation of semantic HTML does not provide enough content description to explain complicated user interface interactions correctly. ARIA (Accessible Rich Internet Applications) serves as the solution when more description is needed beyond semantic HTML. ARIA includes supplementary traits and functions that developers can add to HTML components to enhance accessibility. The addition of role="button" to either a <div> or <span> element indicates meaningful behavioral similarity to buttons, thus enabling screen readers to deliver appropriate announcements to users. Users who depend on assistive technology benefit from ARIA attributes that include aria-live as well as aria-label and aria-expanded because these attributes deliver real-time updates and status information for dynamic elements. Secure, user-friendly standards should be applied before ARIA because they prove essential for developing interactive systems with multiple components.

2.2.3 WCAG Guidelines and Compliance

A set of internationally standardized Web Content Accessibility Guidelines named WCAG exists for enhancing digital content accessibility to people with disabilities. WCAG provides comprehensive guidelines that include instructions for image text alternatives alongside cognitive impairment support for navigation structures. Most websites implement the Web Content Accessibility Guidelines at the Level AA compliance standard, while WCAG provides three different conformance levels: A, AA, and AAA. The web design and development process should follow these guidelines because they help developers create sites that serve all user needs. Website accessibility improves along with legal safety along with user expansion through WCAG compliance implementations.

2.2.4 Alt Text for Images and Multimedia Content

The main part of web accessibility depends on delivering text alternatives to accompany all non-text elements that include images and videos and additional multimedia types. The incorporation of alt attributes in img tags serves as the common mechanism to achieve text alternatives. Trace text provides screen readers the ability to describe image contents, thus enabling visually impaired users to interpret visual information. The wording of alt text must remain direct yet relevant to its subject content in addition to basic descriptions. The development of multimedia content requires alternate descriptions through captions, transcripts, or audio descriptions. These accessibility measures help users understand media content effectively, as they are essential elements of WCAG requirements.

2.2.5 Keyboard Navigation and Focus Management

Accessibility is not just about visual elements—it also encompasses the usability of a website through non-visual means, particularly keyboard navigation. Most website users with disabilities need keyboards combined with assistive tools to browse online platforms because standard mouse operation remains inaccessible for them. Total keyboard operability must exist on every website for accessibility reasons. Correct focus state management must include providing easy access and focusability for interactive components like buttons, links, and form elements through tab key navigation. Developers can also use the tabindex attribute to define the tab order and the focus pseudo-class in CSS to style focused elements, providing visual cues that improve navigation for keyboard users.

2.2.6 Color Contrast and Visual Accessibility

Web accessibility depends greatly on proper color contrast selection, which many developers fail to understand. Users with visual impairments or color blindness, along with other groups, have difficulties perceiving text versus background when contrast ratios remain too low. According to WCAG guidelines, both normal text must meet a 4.5:1 contrast ratio and large text needs at least a 3:1 ratio. The adequate contrast between text and its background enables developers to create readable content for all individuals, including people with low vision. The assessment of website contrast standards becomes simpler through the use of tool-based color contrast checkers. Color on its own should not be used for information communication since text labels or icons with color cues will enhance the accessibility of content.

2.2.7 Forms and Accessible Form Controls

Forms are a key component of many websites, and making them accessible is crucial for ensuring that users with disabilities can submit data effectively. This can be achieved by using proper labels with the <label> tag, associating labels with form controls using the for attribute, and providing clear error messages for validation feedback. Accessible forms also include attributes like aria-required, aria-invalid, and aria-described by to communicate form states and instructions to screen readers.

2.2.8 Responsive Web Design and Accessibility

The core element for contemporary accessibility becomes responsive web design since this approach helps websites automatically adjust according to different device screens. The websites need to provide web content that works well for mobile devices and screen readers and assistive technologies because users access content through those platforms. Web content needs to present information clearly while reducing horizontal scrolling that CSS media queries and HTML5 elements such as <header>, <nav> and <footer> should normalize to achieve. A multichannel accessible website creates better experiences for all visitors through its improvement of universal accessibility, which benefits users with disabilities.

2.2.9 Accessible Tables and Data Presentation

Tables are often used to present complex data, but they can be challenging for users with disabilities if not properly structured. HTML elements must be properly used to make tables accessible, including <th> for headers, <caption> for descriptions, and scope attributes for row or column header designation. For users relying on screen readers, these semantic elements help provide context and meaning to the data. Additionally, ensuring that tables are navigable using the keyboard, with clear focus indicators, is an important part of creating an inclusive design. Developers who follow suitable table accessibility guidelines improve data readability for all user types.

2.2.10 Testing and Validating Accessibility

Testing is essential to validate the implemented accessibility features because it proves that websites fulfill their accessibility standards. A combination of tools consisting of screen readers, including JAWS and NVDA, along with color contrast checkers and keyboard-only navigation testing technologies, supports developers to spot accessibility problems. Additionally, browser extensions like Lighthouse or WAVE provide automated accessibility audits that highlight errors and areas for improvement. However, automated tools should always be supplemented with manual testing to ensure that real users' experiences are accurately represented. Prolonged testing of accessibility enables developers to sustain optimal technical standards, which helps them create platforms usable for a wide spectrum of users.

2.2.11 Creating an Inclusive Web

Web developers can establish sites that become more navigable and user-friendly for users with disabilities by using semantic HTML elements together with ARIA attributes alongside WCAG guidelines. Web development processes must be accessible starting from the design through testing and concluding at launch. Developers should maintain their commitment to accessibility standards because the web's evolution will boost accessibility needs, which makes current best practices mandatory knowledge for all web developers. Every user who has any abilities can access information and services equally on an accessible website.

2.3 Forms, Input Validation, and User Interactions

Web applications use forms as their basic element to let users provide data through multiple operations, which include both registration and login activities as well as survey responses and purchases. The process depends heavily on correct input validation methods. Users are prevented from making mistakes through input validation because it checks that all data satisfies necessary standards before the submission process. Input validation functions at both client and server sides through HTML5, JavaScript, and CSS methods. Client-side validation enables on-the-spot feedback to users, although server-side validation measures data integrity after submission to stop attempted attacks.

2.3.1 Structure of an HTML Form

The <form> element functions as a field group to develop HTML forms. Users can add multiple input options inside the form. Multiple input types inside the form collect user data through it. HTML takes forms from input elements that contain values for text and password boxes as well as number inputs and select dropdowns and buttons for form submission. A form needs the action attribute within its <form> element to indicate the URL destination along with the method attribute to determine the data sending method, which uses POST or GET as standard practices. Every field in the form requires clear labeling in addition to a well-organized layout to guarantee ease of use for all users, particularly users with disabilities.

Table 2.1 Forms, Input Validation, and User Interactions in HTML

Concept	Description
HTML Forms	Uses <form> to collect user input with various elements like <input>, <textarea>, <select>, and <button>
Form Attributes	Includes action, method, enctype, autocomplete, and novalidate to control form behavior
Input Types	Various <input> types like text, email, password, number, date, file, checkbox, and radio for different data inputs
Client-Side Validation	Uses HTML attributes like required, pattern, min, max, and maxlength to enforce input rules before submission
JavaScript Validation	Provides custom validation using JavaScript for dynamic and complex input checks
User Feedback	Uses <output>, JavaScript alerts, or inline messages to give real-time feedback to users
Interactive Elements	Elements like <button>, <details>, <dialog>, and event listeners (onclick, onchange) for dynamic interactions

2.3.2 Input Types and Their Uses

HTML5 introduced a variety of input types that allow developers to capture specific types of data more easily. The email-type input field validates the input data as an email address, while the number-type input only accepts numerical values from the user. Users can choose dates through a built-in calendar interface when they use an input field with type=date. Using the appropriate input types ensures that the data entered is more likely to be in the desired format, reducing errors and the need for complex validation logic.

2.3.3 Client-Side Validation: Basic HTML5 Features

HTML5 brought several new attributes that allow for client-side validation, which means the browser can check the input data before it is sent to the server. Some commonly used attributes include:

- The system demands that users complete the provided input section before allowing the submission process.

- The pattern attribute employs regular expressions to validate how input data should appear for phone numbers and ZIP codes.

• The min and max attributes set quantitative limits for numeric data as well as date fields.

• A text field accepts characters with a maximum length restriction defined through the maxlength attribute.

• The type attribute verifies incoming data matches the specified input format, so type="email" enforces email-address entries, and type="url" controls URL validation.

These attributes provide immediate feedback to users if their input does not meet the specified criteria, improving the overall user experience.

The following is an example of a registration form that combines HTML5 built-in validation with JavaScript for additional checks. The JavaScript ensures that the password and confirm password fields match before submission.

```
<!DOCTYPE html>

<html lang="en">

<head>

    <meta charset="UTF-8">

    <meta name="viewport" content="width=device-width, initial-
          scale=1.0">

    <title>Registration Form</title>

</head>

<body>

    <h2>Registration Form</h2>

    <form id="registrationForm" action="#" method="POST">

        <!-- Name -->

        <label for="name">Full Name:</label>

        <input type="text" id="name" name="name" required minlength="3"
          placeholder="Enter your full name"><br><br>

        <!-- Email -->

        <label for="email">Email:</label>

        <input type="email" id="email" name="email" required
          placeholder="Enter your email"><br><br>

        <!-- Password -->

        <label for="password">Password:</label>

        <input type="password" id="password" name="password" required
          minlength="6" placeholder="Enter your password"><br><br>

        <!-- Confirm Password -->

        <label for="confirmPassword">Confirm Password:</label>

        <input type="password" id="confirmPassword" name="confirmPassword"
          required placeholder="Confirm your password"><br><br>

        <!-- Submit Button -->
```

```
        <button type="submit">Register</button>
    </form>
    <script>
document.getElementById('registrationForm').addEventListener('submit',
          function(event) {
            const password = document.getElementById('password').value;
            const confirmPassword = document.getElementById('confirmPasswo
          rd').value;
            if (password !== confirmPassword) {
                alert("Passwords do not match!");
                event.preventDefault(); // Prevent form submission
            }
        });
    </script>
</body>
</html>
```

2.3.4 Custom Validation with JavaScript

Although HTML5 provides some basic validation features, custom validation often requires JavaScript. This allows for more flexibility in checking complex conditions that cannot be easily handled by HTML alone. JavaScript can listen for form submission events and check whether the data entered into each field matches the expected format, length, or other criteria. If any field is invalid, JavaScript can display a message, highlight the field, or prevent the form from being submitted until the error is corrected.

For example, custom validation can be used to check that two password fields match or that a user enters a valid age (e.g., greater than 18). JavaScript also allows for real-time validation as the user types, providing instant feedback rather than waiting until the form is submitted.

2.3.5 Accessibility Considerations for Forms

It is essential to establish form accessibility for users who have disabilities. Users who access forms using screen readers, along with those who have visual impairments, can effectively use forms when developers employ suitable HTML components together with correct attributes. Screen readers will identify form fields through <label> elements when these items are properly linked together through the for attribute. Within accessible forms, developers need to deliver distinct error notifications about failed validation together with making all fields reachable by keyboard input.

2.3.6 Error Handling and User Feedback

The process of user feedback obtains vital importance during form submission. Users should receive detailed error messages after submitting forms that contain invalid information or empty fields to assist their correction process. Users must receive exact error messages that both explain what went wrong and present it directly ("Password must be at least 8 characters long" and "Please enter a valid email address"). The mistaken form fields normally get marked for user attention using visual indicators with helpful messages shown in close proximity to each field. Additional support comes from changing input field border colors to help users easily locate mistakes.

2.3.7 Preventing Malicious Input and Security

The necessary security element comes from server-side validation, although client-side validation enhances user experience. Users who are driven by malicious intent can evade client-side validation through their modifications of HTML alongside alternative forms of data submission. The server evaluates inputted data to verify its safety and proper format. Specific security principles when dealing with forms consist of SQL injection prevention through escaping inputs as well as the verification of email addresses and URLs together with data sanitization to stop cross-site scripting (XSS) attacks.

2.3.8 Enhancing User Interaction with Form Controls

Users enhance form functionality by incorporating interactive components that include drop-down selections combined with date pickers and checkboxes and radio button groups. The target audience benefits from these elements since they both facilitate data collection for specific types and streamline the form experience with improved navigation. User selection of their country through a dropdown menu proves easier than manual entry of country names for form completion. The interface would both improve and lower the probability of mistakes through custom date selection controls as well as file upload functionality.

2.3.9 Asynchronous Form Submission with AJAX

Web developers submit forms through AJAX (Asynchronous JavaScript and XML) for asynchronous communication during modern web development. The AJAX functionality sends form data to the server without refreshing the entire page, thus resulting in a pleasurable and rapid user experience. Real-time validation results that confirm username availability during registration can be presented through AJAX updates of page sections. The feature makes it possible to develop forms that don't force page reloads during real-time interactions.

2.3.10 Mobile-Friendly Forms

Users need responsive and easy-to-use forms for mobile devices because mobile phones have become mainstream. HTML5 includes tel and email input types, which automatically present the appropriate mobile keyboard, making data entry precise for users.

2.3.11 Best Practices for Form Design and User Interaction

Designing forms for web applications demands meticulous detail work because they represent a fundamental web application component. Improved form creation results from correct HTML elements alongside input validation along with JavaScript technologies. Successful form creation depends on three key elements, including accessibility features combined with real-time feedback provision and mobile compatibility enablements. The combination of these optimal methods produces better user-friendly forms that deliver functional and inclusive forms.

2.4 Integrating Media (Audio, Video, and Graphics)

People nowadays access websites that contain more than plain text through their integration of multimedia elements, including images, audio, and video. Media integration within systems enhances both user experiences along with information retention and allows content to absorb better. With built-in multimedia embedding support through HTML5, users no longer need streaming media plugins, including Flash. This section explores various methods for integrating audio, video, and graphics while ensuring compatibility, performance, and accessibility.

2.4.1 Image Formats and Best Practices

Web-based visual communication depends heavily on images as a communication tool. The selection of appropriate file formats results in substantial effects on web page performance combined with appearance quality. The most standard image file types consist of:

• JPEG functions well with images that contain photographs alongside gradients since it maintains quality during high compression.

• Images that require transparent backgrounds should use PNG because it provides excellent support for transparency effects.

• GIF is a suitable option for animation; however, it functions with restricted color intensity capabilities.

• SVG stands as the vector-based file format that maintains perfect image quality during scaling applications for icons along with logos.

• WebP represents a current image standard that uses its abilities to maintain high-resolution visuals through decreased file dimensions relative to JPEG and PNG formats.

Developers must use TinyPNG or ImageOptim to compress images in addition to implementing srcset and sizes techniques to deliver images that match user devices.

2.4.2 Embedding Images with the <img> Tag

The <img> tag is used to display images on web pages. Example usage:

```
<img src="image.jpg" alt="Descriptive text for accessibility" width="600"
        height="400">
```

- alt Attribute: Provides alternative text for screen readers and improves SEO.
- width & height Attributes: Define the dimensions to prevent layout shifts.
- srcset and sizes: Help serve responsive images based on screen size.

```
<img src="default.jpg" srcset="small.jpg 480w, medium.jpg 1024w, large.
        jpg 1920w" sizes="(max-width: 600px) 480px, (max-width: 1200px)
        1024px, 1920px" alt="Example image">
```

Using CSS for Image Optimization

CSS can be used to control how images appear on a webpage:

```
img {
    max-width: 100%;
    height: auto;
}
```

This ensures that images remain responsive and scale properly on different devices.

2.4.3 SVG Graphics and Their Advantages

The SVG file format enables clear images with independent resolution that developers can modify using CSS and JavaScript. Example of embedding an SVG:

```
<svg width="100" height="100">
    <circle cx="50" cy="50" r="40" stroke="black" stroke-width="3"
          fill="red" />
</svg>
```

Advantages of SVG

- Small file sizes compared to PNGs for icons and logos
- Easily scalable without loss of quality
- Can be animated using CSS or JavaScript

Embedding Audio with the <audio> Tag

HTML5 introduced the <audio> tag for playing sound files without plugins. Example usage:

```
<audio controls>
    <source src="audio.mp3" type="audio/mpeg">
    <source src="audio.ogg" type="audio/ogg">
    Your browser does not support the audio element.
</audio>
```

- ***Controls:*** Displays built-in play, pause, and volume controls.
- ***Multiple <source> elements:*** Ensures compatibility across different browsers.
- ***Fallback text:*** Provides a message if the browser does not support the audio tag.

2.4.4 Advanced Audio Features with JavaScript

For interactive applications, JavaScript can control audio playback:

```
<button onclick="document.getElementById('myAudio').play()">Play Audio</
        button>
<audio id="myAudio" src="audio.mp3"></audio>
```

2.4.5 Embedding Videos with the <video> Tag

Similar to the <audio> tag, the <video> element allows native video playback in modern browsers:

```
<video controls width="600">
    <source src="video.mp4" type="video/mp4">
    <source src="video.webm" type="video/webm">
    Your browser does not support the video tag.
</video>
```

- ***Controls:*** Enables built-in play, pause, and volume control.
- ***Width & height:*** Define the video dimensions.
- ***Multiple <source> elements:*** Ensures compatibility with different formats.

2.4.6 Autoplay, Loop, and Muted Attributes

Additional attributes for the <video> tag:

```
    <video autoplay loop muted>
            <source src="background.mp4" type="video/mp4">
</video>
```

Autoplay: Plays the video automatically when the page loads.

Loop: Repeats the video indefinitely.

Muted: Mutes the video by default (necessary for autoplay in many browsers).

2.4.7 Embedding YouTube and Vimeo Videos

Instead of hosting large video files, developers often embed videos from YouTube or Vimeo:

```
<iframe width="560" height="315" src="https://www.youtube.com/embed/VIDEO_ID" allowfullscreen></iframe>
```

Embedding third-party videos reduces server load and improves performance.

2.4.8 Accessibility and Performance Considerations

When using media, it's essential to consider accessibility and performance:

- ***Provide Alternative Text:*** Use alt attributes for images and captions for videos.
- ***Use Transcripts/Subtitles:*** Provide subtitles using <track> inside <video>.
- ***Lazy Loading:*** Improve page speed by loading media only when needed:

```
<img src="image.jpg" loading="lazy" alt="Lazy-loaded image">
```

- ***Optimize File Sizes:*** Compress images and videos before uploading.
- ***Avoid Autoplay for Critical Content:*** Some users may find autoplay intrusive, so use it wisely.

2.4.9 Best Practices for Media Integration

Integrating media effectively enhances user engagement and provides a richer web experience. Choosing the right formats, optimizing performance, and ensuring accessibility are key to a successful multimedia strategy.

2.5 Performance Optimization Techniques

Your website's slowness causes more people to leave the page rapidly, which results in worse search engine positions and dissatisfied users. The optimization techniques operate to minimize load times and establish faster responsiveness along with making interactions fluid. The performance goals are reached through various techniques that focus on image optimization alongside caching methods and both reduced HTTP requests and code execution efficiency. Acceptable website optimization leads to higher user engagement while simultaneously boosting SEO positions and generating more sales.

2.5.1 Image Optimization for Faster Loading

Page size significantly depends on images that need optimized treatment. The use of contemporary WebP image files instead of conventional PNGs and JPEGs reduces file size substantially without distorting image quality. The utilization of responsive image technology through srcset allows viewers to get images that fit their device screen resolution. TinyPNG and ImageOptim serve as tools for performing file size compression on web pages. The practice of lazy loading allows images to load at a later time only when they come into view, which lessens the time needed for an initial page load. Correct image optimization delivers browsers an efficient browsing experience by enabling smooth operations.

Where:

- Overall cost (optimization objective)
- Distortion (loss of image quality)
- Bit rate (file size)
- Lagrange multiplier (controls trade-off between quality and compression)

This equation helps optimize images for faster loading while maintaining acceptable visual quality.

2.5.2 Minification and Compression of CSS, JavaScript, and HTML

Minification eliminates redundant characters such as spaces, comments, and line breaks from code files throughout HTML, CSS, and JavaScript. File sizes become smaller with a subsequent acceleration of page loading speed. Web developers use the UglifyJS tool for JavaScript files alongside CSSNano as a tool for CSS to execute automated minification functions. Web servers should enable compression methods Gzip or Brotli to decrease file size before they transmit content. The webpages experience faster load times because these methods cut down the volume of data that travels from servers to browsers while adding efficiency to the process.

2.5.3 Reducing HTTP Requests for Improved Performance

Every element on a webpage, including pictures and both scripts and stylesheets, needs its own HTTP request that decreases website loading speed. Compression of requests stands as a vital method for performance enhancement. When CSS and JavaScript files merge into fewer files, it reduces the number of required HTTP requests. The technique of using CSS sprites unites multiple images into one file, which produces fewer requests for small images or icons. The removal of external scripts together with third-party resources can improve website loading efficiency by streamlining the overall process.

2.5.4 Leveraging Browser Caching

The caching function in browsers lets users save frequently requested files directly onto their devices, which minimizes repetitive downloads. A proper cache expiration header in an HTTP response helps maintain the local storage of static files, including images and CSS and JavaScript code, for longer durations. By reducing server load, subsequent page loads get faster. Cache-control mechanisms, such as Expires and ETag, help browsers determine whether they need to request a new version of a file. Proper caching implementation significantly enhances user experience by making web pages load almost instantly on return visits.

2.5.5 Content Delivery Networks (CDN) for Faster Content Delivery

Web content delivery happens through a Content Delivery Network (CDN) system that operates with distributed server networks operating according to user location. CDNs provide better load times by delivering static assets through a nearby server network that also reduces latency. The popular CDN providers Cloudflare, Akamai, and Amazon CloudFront distribute traffic to enable the main server to handle more requests reliably. CDNs are particularly beneficial for global audiences, as they ensure consistent performance regardless of the user's location. Implementing a CDN enhances website speed, reduces bandwidth costs, and increases availability during traffic spikes.

2.5.6 Optimizing JavaScript Execution and Removing Render-Blocking Scripts

Web page loading will become slower because of inadequate JavaScript optimization. The download of lengthy JavaScript files needs to occur asynchronously because this practice stops other page elements from showing during loading. Pages can continue to render normally through the help of the async and defer attributes, which control script execution timing. Unnecessary JavaScript code along with orphaned uses should be removed to decrease processing load. The performance can be improved through the use of efficient frameworks, besides minimizing third-party library dependencies, and through proper event listener optimization. Proper management of JavaScript code leads to smooth interface performance alongside responsive operations free from unnecessary waits.

2.5.7 Implementing Lazy Loading for Images and Videos

The resource loading technique named lazy loading delays unessential assets until required purposes. In lazy loading, only the contents currently visible to users are loaded at first while deferring other content until it becomes relevant. Page loading times decrease substantially at the start because of this technique while service performance appears more immediate. Content loading occurs dynamically when a user scrolls down, thereby preventing unnecessary bandwidth usage. Browser support for native lazy loading exists through the loading="lazy" image attribute together with JavaScript lazy loading solutions for older browser versions. The performance enhancement technique results in higher speeds and better user experience, particularly when dealing with websites featuring abundant content.

2.5.8 Mobile Performance Optimization and Responsive Design

With the increasing use of mobile devices, optimizing websites for mobile performance is essential. Responsive design ensures that content adapts to different screen sizes, providing a seamless experience across devices. Using media queries in CSS allows for flexible layouts, while mobile-first development prioritizes fast loading times on smaller screens. Additionally, reducing large assets, enabling mobile caching, and avoiding unnecessary animations improve responsiveness. Google's PageSpeed Insights and Lighthouse tools help assess mobile performance and suggest improvements. A well-optimized mobile experience is crucial for user engagement and SEO rankings.

2.5.9 Reducing the Use of Redirects

Redirects add additional HTTP requests and increase load times, negatively impacting performance. While some redirects are necessary, excessive redirections should be avoided. Each redirect requires an additional request-response cycle, slowing down the page load. Redirect chains, where one redirect leads to another, should be eliminated to improve efficiency. Using direct URLs and minimizing unnecessary redirects enhances website speed and reduces latency. Ensuring that all internal links point to the final destination URL prevents unnecessary redirection delays and improves overall performance.

2.5.10 Database Optimization for Faster Back-End Performance

Efficient database management plays a vital role in web performance. Reducing database queries, indexing frequently accessed data, and optimizing SQL queries help speed up data retrieval. Caching database results using tools like Redis or Memcached reduces server load and improves response times. Additionally, limiting the use of dynamic queries and using pagination for large datasets prevents performance degradation. Regular database maintenance, such as cleaning up unused tables and optimizing indexes, ensures that queries execute efficiently. Optimized databases enhance both front-end and back-end performance, providing a smoother user experience.

2.5.11 Server and Hosting Optimization for Better Performance

The choice of hosting and server configuration significantly impacts website performance. Using high-performance servers with sufficient resources ensures that traffic spikes do not slow down response times. Enabling HTTP/2 allows for multiplexing, reducing latency by sending multiple requests over a single connection. Optimizing server response times by reducing TTFB (Time to First Byte) and using fast SSD storage improves speed. Load balancing and auto-scaling can distribute traffic efficiently, preventing server overloads. Investing in high-quality hosting solutions ensures reliable, fast-loading websites with minimal downtime.

2.5.12 Testing and Monitoring Website Performance

For optimum website performance, it is necessary to conduct ongoing observation and testing processes. Users can find improvement guidance through Google PageSpeed Insights together with Lighthouse as well as GTmetrix and WebPageTest. Regularly testing loading times, evaluating resource usage, and checking for broken elements help maintain efficiency. Implementing performance budgets ensures that new changes do not negatively impact speed. Real User Monitoring (RUM) helps track actual user interactions and loading times, providing valuable insights for further optimization. Website performance assessments conducted regularly help maintain both the speed and responsiveness of the website along with its efficiency.

2.5.13 Best Practices for Sustained Performance Optimization

Website performance optimization demands regular inspection and adjustment because it represents a continuous process. By focusing on reducing load times, optimizing resources, and leveraging caching techniques, developers can ensure a seamless browsing experience. Mobile optimization, image compression, and script management play a crucial role in enhancing performance. Using CDNs, minimizing HTTP requests, and optimizing databases further contribute to speed improvements. Regular testing with performance analysis tools helps identify areas for enhancement. Prioritizing these best practices results in a highly efficient, user-friendly, and SEO-optimized website, improving overall engagement and conversions.

3 CSS and Frameworks: Designing the Web

3.1 Advanced CSS Selectors and Properties

Advanced CSS selectors and properties enable developers to create highly efficient, maintainable, and visually appealing designs. By leveraging these techniques, web pages achieve a professional-quality aesthetic while maintaining optimal performance. Selectors like :nth-child(), :nth-of-type(), and :not() allow for precise targeting of elements without excessive class usage, improving both the readability and scalability of stylesheets. The :has() pseudo-class, now gaining broader browser support, introduces parent-aware styling, enabling more dynamic layouts without relying on JavaScript.

In addition to selectors, modern CSS properties enhance design flexibility and interactivity. The clamp(), min(), and max() functions provide dynamic responsiveness by defining fluid values for typography, spacing, and layout dimensions. The container queries feature extends responsiveness beyond traditional media queries, allowing elements to adjust styles based on their parent's size rather than the viewport. The use of @layer for cascade control improves stylesheet organization, ensuring predictable styling behavior when managing complex projects.

Advanced layout techniques such as CSS Grid and Flexbox revolutionize page structures by offering intuitive alignment and distribution mechanisms. Properties like grid-template-areas and gap simplify grid layouts, while flex-basis, align-self, and justify-content provide fine-grained control over flexible elements. The combination of scroll-snap-type with scroll-padding enhances user experience by creating smooth, controlled scrolling effects, particularly useful in carousels and one-page applications.

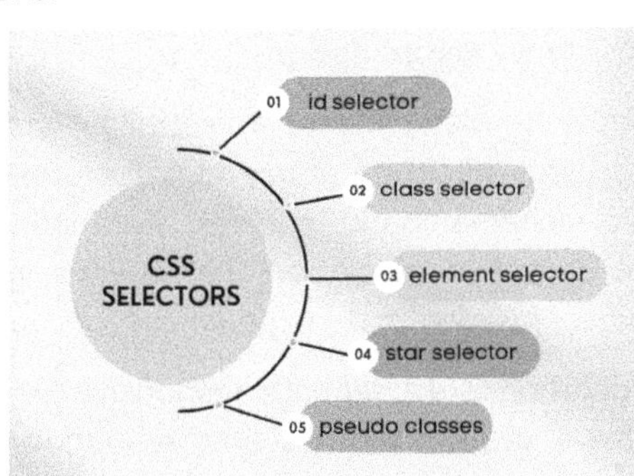

Figure 3.1 Advanced CSS Selectors and Properties

Subtle but impactful visual enhancements are possible through modern styling properties. The backdrop-filter property enables glassmorphism effects, while mask-image and clip-path allow for intricate shape and transparency manipulation. The mix-blend-mode property facilitates creative layering of elements, achieving effects previously limited to graphic design software. CSS variables (--custom-property) streamline theme management by enabling dynamic styling updates with minimal redundancy.

The integration of motion through CSS animations and transitions adds another layer of sophistication. The @keyframes rule combined with animation-timing-function, such as cubic-bezier(), ensures smooth, custom motion effects. The will-change property optimizes rendering performance by signaling intended changes to the browser, reducing layout recalculations, and improving animation smoothness. Hover and focus effects benefit from transition properties that enable seamless state changes, making interactions feel refined and engaging.

These approaches bring benefits to web application aesthetics while maintaining scalability and enhancing maintainability, which are current web application requirements.

3.2 Responsive Web Design with CSS Media Queries

CSS media queries help developers accomplish responsive design by specifying dynamic style application logic that depends on device features, including size dimensions as well as screen quality and user-selected settings such as reduced motion preferences or dark mode options. Through the @media rule, developers can set transitional points that let their site layouts shift automatically without requiring distinct mobile or desktop versions. Responsive design uses three typical breakpoint categories for screens smaller than 600px as well as 600px–1024px and screens bigger than 1024px, while current approaches rely on min-width and max-width parameters.

Flexible layouts using CSS Grid and Flexbox complement media queries by allowing content to reflow dynamically. Properties like display: grid, grid-template-columns, and auto-fit enable layouts to scale effortlessly, while flex-wrap: wrap and justify-content in Flexbox distribute elements based on available space. The use of clamp(), min(), and max() functions ensures fluid typography and spacing without abrupt shifts between breakpoints. Aspect ratio maintains proportional scaling of elements, preventing distortion when resizing.

Container queries represent the next evolution in responsiveness by enabling elements to adjust based on their parent container rather than the viewport. This approach enhances modularity, allowing components to remain self-contained and adaptable in various layouts. Combined with CSS variables (--custom-property), container-based styling improves maintainability and consistency across designs.

Beyond layout, media queries cater to accessibility and user preferences. The (prefers-reduced-motion) query helps minimize animations for users sensitive to motion, improving inclusivity. (prefers-color-scheme: dark) enables automatic dark mode styling, enhancing readability in low-light environments. Additional queries like (orientation: portrait), (hover: none), and (pointer: coarse) help optimize experiences for touch-based and mobile users.

Performance considerations are essential in responsive design. Efficient use of loading="lazy" for images and responsive srcset attributes ensures optimal asset delivery based on screen resolution. CSS properties like image-set() adapt images to different pixel densities, reducing bandwidth usage on high-DPI displays. Combining media queries with modern layout techniques,

Table 3.1 Responsive Web Design: CSS Media Queries Cheat Sheet

Topic	Description	Example	Usage
Media Query Syntax	Defines breakpoints for responsive styles	@media (max-width: 600px) { }	Apply styles for small screens
Min & Max Width	Targets specific screen widths	@media (min-width: 768px) and (max-width: 1024px) { }	Tablet-specific styles
Viewport Meta Tag	Ensures proper scaling on mobile devices	<meta name="viewport" content="width=device-width, initial-scale=1">	Required for responsiveness
Flexbox & Grid	Flexible layout techniques for responsiveness	display: flex; or display: grid;	Create dynamic layouts
Mobile-First Design	Starts styling for mobile before larger screens	Default CSS for small screens, add media queries for larger ones	Efficient, modern approach
Common Breakpoints	Standard screen widths for media queries	480px, 768px, 1024px, 1280px	Targets different device sizes
Orientation Queries	Adapts styles based on landscape/portrait mode	@media (orientation: landscape) { }	Enhances usability
Dark Mode Support	Adjusts styles for light/dark themes	@media (prefers-color-scheme: dark) { }	Improves accessibility
Performance Considerations	Avoids excessive media queries for efficiency	Use responsive units (%, em, rem) instead of fixed px	Enhances speed & maintainability

progressive enhancement strategies, and accessibility-conscious styling ensures a seamless, professional-quality user experience across all devices and contexts.

3.3 CSS Grid and Flexbox for Layouts

Developers possess CSS Grid and Flexbox as powerful layout systems, enabling them to create responsive and complex designs through tools that eliminate the requirement of floats or complex positioning. The two systems generate adaptable design structures yet operate best at different implementation instances.

Two-dimensional CSS Grid works across both vertical and horizontal directions to build elaborate grid frameworks. CSS Grid serves layouts that require item organization across both horizontal and vertical axes without compromise because of its suitability in full-page designs as well as complex dashboards and galleries. Developers can utilize grid-template-areas in CSS Grid to generate area maps through basic syntax, which facilitates better understanding and arrangement of elements throughout the grid structure. The auto-fill and auto-fit functions allow automatic column/row resizing through available space, thus maintaining design flexibility for different screen sizes.

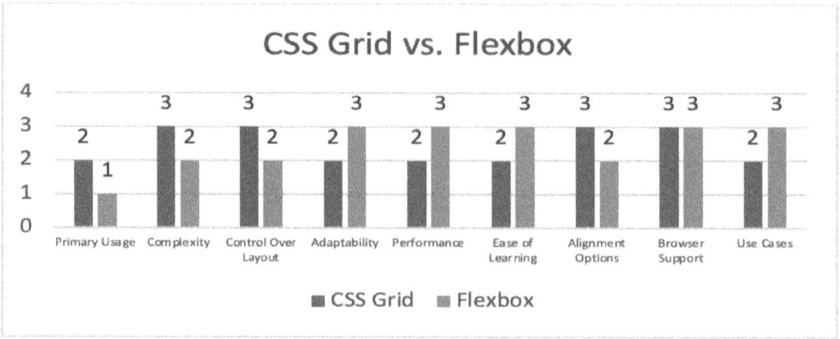

Figure 3.2 CSS Grid vs. Flexbox

The one-dimensional layout system Flexbox provides a vertical or horizontal arrangement of elements using a single axis. The system performs best to manage element positioning and placement, particularly when working on navigation bars, form inputs, or image galleries. Users can use justify-content together with align-items and align-self properties to distribute space uniformly between elements in Flexbox. Alignable layouts achieve their maximum utility from the flex-grow, flex-shrink, and flex-basis properties integrated within Flexbox because these properties enable custom item scaling to handle available space.

One of the key advantages of CSS Grid and Flexbox is their ability to work together in harmony. Developers can use Grid for large-scale layouts and Flexbox for smaller components within those grids. For instance, you might use Grid to lay out a multi-column page, and within those columns, use Flexbox to arrange items like headers, buttons, and images. This combination ensures that you can create layouts that are both highly structured and responsive, all while maintaining clean and maintainable code.

Responsive functionality is present in both systems through their included features. Media queries linked with grid-template-columns and grid-template-rows enable you to modify the grid structure naturally through different screen sizes using Grid. You can create flexible responsive designs through simple efforts by using Flexbox features, which include easy order reordering and element wrapping triggered by screen width using flex-wrap.

Incorporating advanced features like minmax(), clamp(), and max-content can further enhance the flexibility of Grid and Flexbox, ensuring your layout adapts intelligently to content and viewport changes. The introduction of subgrid in CSS Grid adds another layer of flexibility by allowing grid items to inherit the layout of their parent grid, which improves consistency across complex designs.

Ultimately, both CSS Grid and Flexbox enable developers to create sophisticated, responsive layouts with ease, and their complementary nature means you can use them in tandem for optimal results in modern web design.

3.4 Preprocessors: SASS and LESS

The popular CSS preprocessors SASS (Syntactically Awesome Stylesheets) together with LESS enable developers to enhance standard CSS functionality with valuable enhancements including variables as well as nesting and mixins and functions. CSS preprocessors such as SASS and LESS eliminate complicated styling issues through tools that simplify the management of large CSS project development. The main benefit you get from preprocessors enables developers to create reusable and maintainable code blocks, which ultimately enhances team output while allowing future expansion of your project.

Developers who use SASS benefit from its role as a popular CSS preprocessor to establish variables that remove the necessity to duplicate design code multiple times. The nesting feature of these preprocessors allows developers to arrange CSS rules in a hierarchical order, thus creating more readable and easier-to-manage code. SASS enables developers to apply conditional styling through its control directives, including @if and @else, combined with specified conditions.

LESS features a syntax that resembles CSS syntax while sharing many characteristics with SASS, therefore providing developers with an easier pathway to migrate from standard CSS coding. The programming features of LESS include variable support, mixins, and nesting, although it does not contain the advanced capabilities that SASS provides, such as loops and functions. LESS continues to be widely adopted as a preprocessing language because of its user-friendly nature while still working within typical CSS development procedures. They enable development through preprocessors until the program generates regular CSS code, which browsers process and work with traditional CSS files without issues.

Steps for preprocessing LESS and SASS files can be automated by integrating them with different build tools, which include Gulp and Webpack. The development process becomes easier when code autocompilation and refreshing occur automatically as developers modify their work. Your development workflow gains efficiency through the processor integration because developers can create modular code effortlessly without handling direct compilation or code duplication.

In addition to improving code maintainability, using SASS or LESS encourages better organization and the adoption of best practices in web development. By embracing features like variables, mixins, and partials, developers can create reusable components, significantly reducing the redundancy in CSS code and improving collaboration between team members. Furthermore, these preprocessors allow for more efficient collaboration by facilitating the creation of style guides and shared design systems.

3.4.1 How Do SASS and LESS Differ in Terms of Features?

SASS and LESS both serve as CSS preprocessors but differ primarily in their feature sets and syntax. SASS is more feature-rich, offering advanced programming concepts such as loops, functions, conditionals (@if, @else), and inheritance, which allow for more dynamic and complex styling rules. It also supports two syntaxes: the indented syntax (without curly braces) and the SCSS syntax (similar to regular CSS). LESS, on the other hand, has a simpler syntax closer to standard CSS, which makes it easier for developers to transition. LESS lacks advanced features like loops and functions but still offers basic features like variables, mixins, and nesting.

3.4.2 What Benefits Do Variables and Mixins Offer When Working with Preprocessors?

Variables in preprocessors like SASS and LESS allow developers to store values such as colors, fonts, and dimensions, ensuring consistency throughout the stylesheet. This reduces the chances of errors, such as having mismatched colors across the site. Mixins, on the other hand, allow for reusable chunks of code, which can be included in multiple places in the stylesheet. They reduce redundancy, improve code maintainability, and make it easier to update styles globally without modifying individual rules. With mixins, you can even create complex rules that accept parameters, further enhancing their flexibility.

3.4.3 How Can Integrating Preprocessors into a Workflow Improve Development Efficiency?

Development workflows gain considerable efficiency benefits when they integrate SASS or LESS because compilation and CSS minification happen automatically. Task runners, including Gulp and Webpack, enable developers to achieve automatic compilation of preprocessor files that maintains an up-to-date final CSS version. The automation system reduces the time needed for compilation command execution and removes tedious manual tasks. When code becomes modular and reusable it leads to shorter periods of debugging together with decreasing time needed for style maintenance.

3.4.4 What Is the Role of a Preprocessor in Modern Web Design?

A preprocessor in modern web design acts as an enhanced version of CSS, offering features like variables, nesting, and mixins that make CSS code more maintainable, efficient, and scalable. Preprocessors allow developers to write cleaner, more organized stylesheets that are easier to manage, especially for large projects. They also help create more dynamic and adaptable designs, as they allow for conditional styling and code reuse. In a fast-paced development environment, using a preprocessor can streamline the styling process and enable teams to collaborate more effectively on consistent design systems.

3.4.5 How Does SASS Improve the Scalability and Maintainability of CSS Code?

SASS enhances system scalability through its tools that let developers divide CSS styles into modular segments called partials for reusable and maintainable application design. SASS enables developers to enforce DRY principles through its nesting abilities combined with variables, mixins, and functions. Using modular design methods is highly beneficial for extensive applications because it enables the effective management of complicated style structures. SASS simplifies project growth by maintaining organizational structure together with decreasing duplicated code, which lets developers adjust to design updates without difficulties.

3.5 CSS Frameworks (Bootstrap, Tailwind, Material Design)

Using these frameworks helps developers construct quick, responsive websites with good looks through pre-made style components that spare developers from long CSS development. Each framework has distinct strengths alongside its unique framework design, along with its own development tools, making them appropriate for different applications.

Bootstrap stands as the most popular CSS framework that provides developers with pre-designed components, which include buttons as well as navigation bars, forms, modals, and grids. The 12-column grid system of Bootstrap functions from mobile devices first while allowing users to generate responsive layouts. Roman Script provides its users with JavaScript plugins that work alongside carousels along with tooltips and dropdowns to enhance functionality. Bootstraps, easy accessibility, and its vast user community stand out as primary benefits because developers can easily locate support as well as solutions to their problems. The built-in pre-made components of this system lead to identical web page appearances until specific customizations are implemented.

Tailwind CSS uses a distinct utility-first framework to achieve its operational model. Tailwind provides developers with fundamental utility classes (p-4 bg-blue-500 text-center), which empower them to construct personalized designs through these components. The system provides developers with superior control of design elements because they have the ability to handle design tasks directly instead of being limited to preordained components. Tablewind enables developers to create more flexible, maintainable layouts because developers can customize their styles by building their styles with its utility components. The flexibility of Tailwind suits projects that must create distinctive designs because it takes additional initial work but avoids duplicate development from existing design foundations.

Material Design from Google delivers a standardized contemporary interface language that develops user-friendly interfaces that users can easily understand. Material Design provides a complete package with UX guidelines in addition to animation rules as well as transition principles and CSS functionalities. This design system presents a collection of pre-designed features that include buttons, cards, and icons together with navigation elements. These components follow operational standards developed by Google. Tailwind provides users with enhanced flexibility compared to Material Design because its strict design rules restrict customization options, although this framework works well as a design foundation.

The main benefit of using a CSS framework is the speed with which developers can create responsive, consistent designs. These frameworks also help enforce best practices in terms of layout and accessibility. However, developers may need to balance using a framework with the need for customization. For example, while Bootstrap can save time, it may lead to websites looking generic unless tailored. On the other hand, Tailwind offers more freedom and uniqueness but requires a deeper understanding of the utility-first approach. Material Design provides strong consistency and adherence to design principles but may feel restrictive in certain design scenarios.

In choosing the right framework, developers should consider project requirements, team familiarity, and long-term maintainability. If speed and consistency are key, Bootstrap or Material Design may be ideal. If customization and a unique design are essential, Tailwind might be the best choice.

3.5.1 What Is the Primary Difference Between Bootstrap and Tailwind CSS in Terms of Design Approach?

The main separation exists between Bootstrap and Tailwind CSS regarding design methodology. Bootstrap delivers predesigned components, which include buttons, grids, and forms inside a predefined component-based structure. Speedy layout creation becomes possible through this approach but requires designers to design around already available components unless they customize them. Through its utility-first method Tailwind CSS provides basic utility classes that developers can use to build custom designs by combining p-4, bg-blue-500, and text-center classes. The framework gives developers greater freedom to control appearance along with increased design effort that takes longer to create layouts.

Bootstrap follows a component-based approach, providing pre-designed UI elements like buttons, modals, and grids that ensure a consistent look with minimal effort. In contrast, Tailwind CSS uses a utility-first approach, where developers apply low-level utility classes directly to elements, offering greater flexibility and customization without enforcing a predefined design system. Bootstrap is ideal for quick prototyping with a consistent style, whereas Tailwind is better for fully custom designs with optimized CSS usage.

Design Approach = (Pre-styled Components) – (Utility-First Classes)

3.5.2 How Does Tailwind's Utility-First Approach Benefit Developers Compared to Traditional Frameworks?

Tailwind's utility-first approach benefits developers by providing greater flexibility and control over the design process. Instead of being restricted to predefined components, developers can use a wide range of utility classes to style individual elements. This allows for custom, unique designs without having to start from scratch or override pre-existing styles. Additionally, utility classes make the code more modular, as developers can easily apply or adjust styles directly in the HTML without having to navigate large CSS files. This approach can reduce CSS file size and improve maintainability, especially for large projects.

3.5.3 What Are the Key Advantages of Using Material Design for a Web Project?

Material Design offers several key advantages, primarily focused on creating visually cohesive and user-friendly interfaces. The framework follows a set of well-defined design principles, providing consistency across different platforms and devices. Material Design ensures that components such as buttons, cards, and navigation are not only aesthetically pleasing but also optimized for usability and accessibility. Additionally, it includes guidelines for animations, transitions, and spacing, which contribute to a polished user experience. For developers, Material Design offers a comprehensive toolkit for building modern, intuitive web applications with less effort on design decisions.

3.5.4 In What Scenarios Would Bootstrap be More Appropriate than Tailwind CSS?

Bootstrap would be more appropriate than Tailwind CSS in scenarios where quick development and consistency are paramount. If a developer needs to rapidly prototype a website or application with common components (such as forms, navbars, and buttons) and requires a mobile-first, responsive layout, Bootstrap provides an easy-to-use, comprehensive solution. It's ideal for projects where time constraints or standardized design are more important than creating highly customized, unique designs. Additionally, Bootstrap is well-suited for teams or individuals who may not want to spend time creating custom design components from scratch.

3.5.5 How Can Customization Impact the Use of CSS Frameworks like Bootstrap or Material Design?

The method of customization produces major effects when developers use Bootstrap or Material Design frameworks. The pre-designed components and standardized styles exist within both frameworks without being mandatory for customization. Through customization, developers obtain the ability to revise various design components such as colors and typography as well as spacing to fulfill project guidelines and brand identity requirements. However, extensive customization might require overriding default styles or writing additional custom CSS, which could lead to larger file sizes or inconsistent code. In some cases, this can negate the time-saving benefits of using a framework in the first place. In frameworks like Material Design, customization may be more challenging due to its strict design guidelines, potentially limiting flexibility. Conversely, frameworks like Bootstrap can be easily customized through themes or variables, making them a more adaptable choice for many developers.

3.6 Animations and Transitions for Enhanced User Experience

Through animations along with transitions, users experience enhanced UX by receiving visual cues and having better interactivity between their actions and the website/application elements.

Through proper animation, users receive guidance, which helps them view crucial elements and indicates program modifications while simultaneously making interface elements more dynamic and engaging for users to interact with.

Through CSS animations, developers get full control to generate various smooth motion effects in their projects, ranging from fades to slides, rotations, and scaling effects. Through the @keyframes rule, users gain full control of animation timeline development by establishing various states of animation. Developers adjust animation characteristics through three properties: animation-duration to specify timing and animation-timing-function to establish the pace together with animation-delay to determine the sequence of animation activation. The opacity property can be utilized for fading effects, whereas transform properties enable element sliding movements during animations. Through animation programming, interfaces can obtain an added elegant dimension for user interactions, thus creating a more active interface experience.

CSS transitions, on the other hand, are simpler and more focused on changes between two states. Transitions are triggered when an element undergoes a change in state, such as when a user hovers over a button, clicks a link, or focuses on a form input. The transition effect is defined by specifying a property to animate, such as background-color, transform, or height, and setting the transition duration to control how quickly the change occurs. The transition-timing-function allows for customization of the transition's pacing, whether you want it to be linear, ease-in, ease-out, or use a custom timing function like cubic-bezier(). Transitions are often used for hover effects, revealing hidden elements, or smoothly transitioning between different UI states.

The code below uses transitions to develop a gradual transition effect for buttons during mouse hovers. During hover, the button background transforms while simultaneously progressively enlarging its dimensions. The feedback function begins instantly after user interaction and increases system responsiveness. The code should be placed within the section where you explain CSS transitions in your content. The code explains how transition animations smoothly transform a basic two-state change, such as a button hover.

```
.button {
  background-color: #3498db;
  color: white;
  padding: 10px 20px;
  border: none;
  cursor: pointer;
  transition: background-color 0.3s ease, transform 0.3s ease;
}
.button:hover {
  background-color: #2c8fbd;
  transform: scale(1.1);
}
```

Animations and transitions, when used appropriately, enhance the overall usability and aesthetics of a website. They can improve clarity by subtly drawing attention to specific elements or transitions, such as a modal window appearing with a fade or slide effect, helping users navigate the content with ease. Additionally, animations can guide users through processes, like onboarding tutorials or loading indicators, signaling that the system is actively processing information. Thoughtful use of motion also contributes to the overall tone and personality of a website. For example, playful animations may be used in a creative project, while more subdued, smooth transitions are appropriate for a professional or corporate site.

However, it's crucial to use animations and transitions judiciously. Excessive or overly flashy animations can distract users and lead to a negative experience, especially on slower devices or when users have motion sensitivities. The prefers-reduced-motion media query, part of the modern web standards, helps ensure that users who experience discomfort with animations can disable them entirely. By respecting this user preference, you ensure that your design is more inclusive and accessible to all.

Overall, animations and transitions are powerful tools for enhancing user experience, providing a seamless flow from one interaction to another, and making web interfaces more visually appealing and engaging. By carefully considering their application and impact on performance and accessibility, developers can craft websites that are not only functional but also delightful to use.

3.6.1 How Do CSS Animations Differ from Transitions in Terms of Functionality?

CSS animations are more complex than transitions and allow for the continuous change of multiple states over time. They can run indefinitely or loop through a series of keyframes, offering more control over the timing, direction, and duration of an effect. CSS animations are defined using @keyframes to specify multiple states and their transitions. On the other hand, CSS transitions are simpler and trigger only when an element changes between two distinct states (e.g., hover, active, focus). Transitions are best suited for effects that occur once, like changing a button's color on hover. While animations can create more dynamic, multi-step effects, transitions are often used for simple, single-state changes.

3.6.2 Why Is it Important to Consider Accessibility when Using Animations and Transitions?

It's crucial to consider accessibility when using animations and transitions because excessive movement or motion can be disorienting or even harmful to users with certain conditions, such as vestibular disorders or motion sensitivities. Animations can cause discomfort or even trigger symptoms like dizziness or nausea. To address this, developers should respect the prefers-reduced-motion media query, which allows users to disable animations or transitions. The integration of this method allows designers to create accessible layouts that benefit users with poor visual sensitivity along with maintaining visual appeal for other users.

3.6.3 In What Scenarios Would You Use a CSS Animation Instead of a Transition?

CSS animations are ideal for scenarios where you need more complex, multi-step movements or when the animation should repeat or loop. For example, you would use an animation for continuous effects like a loading spinner, an image carousel, or a bouncing element. Animations are also useful when you want to define keyframes to transition through several states over time, such as fading between different colors or scaling an element through various sizes. On the other hand, transitions are better for simpler effects that happen once, like hovering over a button to change its background color or showing a tooltip when an element is focused.

3.6.4 How Can the Prefers-Reduced-Motion Media Query Improve the User Experience?

Users who need reduced motion benefit from the prefers-reduced-motion media query, which enables them to deactivate visual effects across their devices. Users who activate the prefers-reduced-motion query receive static alternatives for animations and transitions, which enhance their experience because of motion sensitivities. When users enable reduced motion, the modal would present without movement instead of playing its typical animation-based sliding effect. The accessibility feature supports user control over their website interaction without discomfort while they navigate web content, thereby enhancing the overall accessibility.

3.6.5 What Role Do Animations and Transitions Play in Guiding User Behavior on a Website?

Animations and transitions play a key role in guiding user behavior by visually indicating changes, providing feedback, and emphasizing important elements. For example, subtle animations can draw attention to critical actions, such as a call-to-action button or a newly loaded section of content. Transitions can guide users through multi-step processes, like form submissions or navigation between pages, by signaling a smooth shift between states. Animations also help users understand system feedback, such as showing a loading spinner while waiting for data or indicating a success message when a form is submitted. These visual cues make interfaces feel more intuitive and engaging, enhancing overall user satisfaction and interaction.

1. Simple Web Page with Styled Heading and Paragraph

```
<!DOCTYPE html>
<html lang="en">
<head>
  <meta charset="UTF-8">
  <title>Simple Page</title>
  <style>
    body {
      font-family: Arial, sans-serif;
      background-color: #f3f4f6;
      margin: 20px;
    }
    h1 {
      color: #1f2937;
    }
    p {
      color: #4b5563;
    }
  </style>
</head>
```

```
<body>
  <h1>Welcome to My Page</h1>
  <p>This is a simple HTML and CSS example.</p>
</body>
</html>
```

2. Basic Responsive Card Layout

```
<!DOCTYPE html>
<html lang="en">
<head>
  <meta charset="UTF-8">
  <title>Card Layout</title>
  <style>
    body {
      font-family: sans-serif;
      background: #f0f0f0;
      padding: 40px;
    }
    .card {
      background: white;
      border-radius: 10px;
      box-shadow: 0 4px 8px rgba(0,0,0,0.1);
      padding: 20px;
      max-width: 300px;
      margin: auto;
    }
    .card h2 {
      margin-top: 0;
    }
    .card p {
      color: #555;
    }
  </style>
</head>
<body>
```

```
  <div class="card">
    <h2>Profile</h2>
    <p>This is a basic card component with padding and shadow.</p>
  </div>
</body>
</html>
```

3. Navigation Bar Example

```
<!DOCTYPE html>
<html lang="en">
<head>
  <meta charset="UTF-8">
  <title>Navbar</title>
  <style>
    body {
      margin: 0;
      font-family: Arial, sans-serif;
    }
    .navbar {
      background-color: #333;
      overflow: hidden;
    }
    .navbar a {
      float: left;
      display: block;
      color: white;
      text-align: center;
      padding: 14px 20px;
      text-decoration: none;
    }
    .navbar a:hover {
      background-color: #ddd;
      color: black;
    }
  </style>
```

```
</head>
<body>
  <div class="navbar">
    <a href="#">Home</a>
    <a href="#">About</a>
    <a href="#">Contact</a>
  </div>
</body>
</html>
```

4. CSS Button Hover Effect

```
<!DOCTYPE html>
<html lang="en">
<head>
  <meta charset="UTF-8">
  <title>Button Hover</title>
  <style>
    .btn {
      background-color: #007bff;
      color: white;
      padding: 10px 20px;
      border: none;
      border-radius: 5px;
      cursor: pointer;
      transition: background-color 0.3s ease;
    }
    .btn:hover {
      background-color: #0056b3;
    }
  </style>
</head>
<body>
  <button class="btn">Click Me</button>
</body>
</html>
```

5. Responsive Login Form

```
<!DOCTYPE html>
<html lang="en">
<head>
  <meta charset="UTF-8">
  <title>Login Form</title>
  <style>
    body {
      background-color: #e0f7fa;
      display: flex;
      justify-content: center;
      align-items: center;
      height: 100vh;
      font-family: sans-serif;
    }
    .login-container {
      background: white;
      padding: 30px;
      border-radius: 10px;
      box-shadow: 0 4px 10px rgba(0,0,0,0.1);
      width: 300px;
    }
    .login-container h2 {
      text-align: center;
      margin-bottom: 20px;
    }
    .login-container input[type="text"],
    .login-container input[type="password"] {
      width: 100%;
      padding: 10px;
      margin: 8px 0;
      border-radius: 5px;
      border: 1px solid #ccc;
    }
    .login-container button {
```

```
      width: 100%;
      padding: 10px;
      background-color: #0288d1;
      border: none;
      color: white;
      border-radius: 5px;
      font-size: 16px;
      cursor: pointer;
    }
    .login-container button:hover {
      background-color: #0277bd;
    }
  </style>
</head>
<body>

<div class="login-container">
  <h2>Login</h2>
  <input type="text" placeholder="Username" />
  <input type="password" placeholder="Password" />
  <button>Login</button>
</div>
</body>
</html>
```

6. Animated Loading Spinner

```
<!DOCTYPE html>
<html lang="en">
<head>
  <meta charset="UTF-8">
  <title>Loading Spinner</title>
  <style>
    body {
      background: #222;
      display: flex;
```

```
      justify-content: center;
      align-items: center;
      height: 100vh;
    }
    .spinner {
      border: 8px solid #f3f3f3;
      border-top: 8px solid #00bcd4;
      border-radius: 50%;
      width: 80px;
      height: 80px;
      animation: spin 1s linear infinite;
    }
    @keyframes spin {
      to { transform: rotate(360deg); }
    }
  </style>
</head>
<body>
<div class="spinner"></div>
</body>
</html>
```

7. Responsive Image Gallery (Grid)

```
<!DOCTYPE html>
<html lang="en">
<head>
  <meta charset="UTF-8">
  <title>Image Gallery</title>
  <style>
    body {
      font-family: Arial;
      margin: 0;
      padding: 20px;
      background: #fafafa;
    }
```

```
    .gallery {
      display: grid;
      grid-template-columns: repeat(auto-fit, minmax(150px, 1fr));
      gap: 15px;
    }
    .gallery img {
      width: 100%;
      border-radius: 8px;
      transition: transform 0.3s ease;
    }
    .gallery img:hover {
      transform: scale(1.05);
    }
  </style>
</head>
<body>

<h2>Image Gallery</h2>
<div class="gallery">
  <img src="https://via.placeholder.com/300" alt="Gallery Image">
  <img src="https://via.placeholder.com/300" alt="Gallery Image">
  <img src="https://via.placeholder.com/300" alt="Gallery Image">
  <img src="https://via.placeholder.com/300" alt="Gallery Image">
</div>

</body>
</html>
```

8. Simple To-Do List UI

```
<!DOCTYPE html>
<html lang="en">
<head>
  <meta charset="UTF-8">
  <title>To-Do List</title>
 <style>
```

```
  body {
    font-family: Arial;
    background: #f0f4f8;
    display: flex;
    justify-content: center;
    padding-top: 60px;
  }
  .todo-container {
    background: white;
    padding: 20px;
    width: 300px;
    border-radius: 10px;
    box-shadow: 0 4px 10px rgba(0,0,0,0.1);
  }
  .todo-container h2 {
    margin: 0 0 15px;
  }
  input[type="text"] {
    width: 100%;
    padding: 10px;
    margin-bottom: 10px;
    border-radius: 5px;
    border: 1px solid #ccc;
  }
  ul {
    list-style: none;
    padding: 0;
  }
  ul li {
    background: #e3f2fd;
    margin: 5px 0;
    padding: 8px 10px;
    border-radius: 4px;
  }
</style>
```

```
</head>
<body>

<div class="todo-container">
  <h2>My To-Do List</h2>
  <input type="text" placeholder="New task..." />
  <ul>
    <li>Buy groceries</li>
    <li>Finish project</li>
  </ul>
</div>
</body>
</html>
```

4 JavaScript: The Dynamic Web

4.1 Modern JavaScript Syntax (ES6+ Features)

Modern JavaScript syntax, introduced with ES6 and subsequent versions, brought several new features that greatly improved the language's efficiency, readability, and functionality. One of the most important changes was the introduction of let and const for variable declarations, replacing the older var keyword. This allows for better scoping and helps avoid common mistakes in variable declarations. Additionally, arrow functions (=>) were introduced to simplify function syntax and retain the context of this from their surrounding code.

Another key feature is the template literals, which allow for easier string interpolation, making it more convenient to work with strings that include variables or expressions. ES6 also introduced destructuring, which simplifies the process of extracting values from arrays or objects and assigning them to variables in a single line of code.

Development teams use the spread operator (...) to make array and object copying and combination operations easy and split their contents into multiple sections. The introduction of Promises simplified asynchronous code execution by simplifying tasks that involve asynchronous operations, including network requests, but eliminating the need for callback functions that would result in complicated, hard-to-maintain code.

The ES6+ standard introduced classes that serve as a mechanism to create defined objects with inheritance handling in JavaScript. Through this update,

Figure 4.1 Modern JavaScript Syntax (ES6+ Features)

JavaScript received an object-oriented approach that simplifies development for programmers who use object-oriented languages.

4.1.1 What Is the Difference Between let and const?

let and const are both used to declare variables in JavaScript, but they differ in their behavior:

• let allows you to reassign a variable after it is declared. For example, you can update its value or reassign it to a different object or array.

• const is used for variables that should not be reassigned. Once you assign a value to a const variable, you cannot reassign it to a different value. However, this only applies to the variable binding itself—if the value is an object or array, its contents can still be modified.

4.1.2 How Do Template Literals Improve String Manipulation in JavaScript?

Template literals allow for easier and more readable string manipulation by enabling string interpolation. Instead of concatenating strings with +, you can embed variables or expressions directly within the string using ${} syntax. This leads to cleaner and more readable code. For example:

```
let name = "Alice";

let greeting = `Hello, ${name}!`; // Instead of 'Hello, ' + name + '!'
```

4.1.3 What Is Destructuring, and How Is it Useful in JavaScript?

Destructuring is a shorthand syntax for extracting values from arrays or objects and assigning them to variables. It simplifies the process of working with data structures like arrays and objects. For example:

```
// Array Destructuring

const [first, second] = [1, 2];

console.log(first, second); // 1, 2

// Object Destructuring

const person = { name: "John", age: 30 };

const { name, age } = person;

console.log(name, age); // "John", 30
```

This makes it easier to work with complex data structures and can lead to more concise code.

4.1.4 What Are Promises, and How Do They Help with Asynchronous Programming?

Asynchrony management through JavaScript is achieved by promises. Promises represent either successful completion or unsuccessful termination of a non-blocking operation that contains its produced outcome. A Promise maintains one status among pending, fulfilled, or rejected states. Promises help simplify the handling of asynchronous code through the elimination of callback hell that happens due to deeply nested callbacks. For example:

```
let myPromise = new Promise((resolve, reject) => {

  let success = true;

  if (success) {
```

```
    resolve("Operation succeeded!");
  } else {
    reject("Operation failed.");
  }
});
myPromise.then(result => console.log(result)).catch(error => console.
          log(error));
```

4.1.5 How Do Classes in ES6 Improve Object-Oriented Programming in JavaScript?

ES6 introduced class syntax to JavaScript, which brings a more structured and object-oriented approach to the language. Classes make it easier to create objects and handle inheritance. They encapsulate data and behavior together and provide a clearer, more readable way to define constructors, methods, and inheritance compared to the old prototype-based approach. For example:

```
class Animal {
  constructor(name) {
    this.name = name;
  }
  speak() {
    console.log(`${this.name} makes a sound.`);
  }
}
class Dog extends Animal {
  speak() {
    console.log(`${this.name} barks.`);
  }
}
let dog = new Dog("Buddy");
dog.speak(); // "Buddy barks."
```

Classes make object-oriented programming in JavaScript more intuitive, especially for developers coming from other OOP languages like Java or C#.

4.2 DOM Manipulation and Event Handling

The essential web development techniques in JavaScript include DOM Modification and Event Response Management. Through these web development tools, users can dynamically exchange and change web page content while making interactive responses to mouse and keyboard activities.

4.2.1 DOM Manipulation

The DOM (Document Object Model) is an interface that allows you to access and manipulate

HTML elements and the structure of a webpage. JavaScript provides several methods for manipulating the DOM:

- ***Selecting Elements:*** You can use methods like document.getElementById(), document.getElementsByClassName(), document.querySelector(), and document.querySelectorAll() to select elements from the DOM.

```
let element = document.getElementById("myElement");
```

- ***Modifying Content:*** Once you've selected an element, you can modify its content using properties like innerHTML, innerText, or textContent.

```
element.innerHTML = "New content!";
```

- ***Changing Styles:*** You can modify the style of an element directly via the style property.

```
element.style.color = "blue";

element.style.fontSize = "20px";
```

- ***Adding/Removing Elements:*** JavaScript also allows you to add or remove elements dynamically using methods like appendChild(), removeChild(), and createElement().

```
let newDiv = document.createElement("div");

document.body.appendChild(newDiv);
```

Event Handling: JavaScript enables developers to handle webpage events through event listeners attached to individual DOM elements. The ability to make webpages interactive is achieved through JavaScript.

- ***Adding Event Listeners:*** Use addEventListener() to listen for specific events on elements and define the callback function to run when the event occurs.

```
element.addEventListener("click", function() {

  alert("Element clicked!");

});
```

- ***Event Types:*** Events can be mouse-based (e.g., click, mouseover), keyboard-based (e.g., keydown, keyup), form-based (e.g., submit, change), and more.

```
element.addEventListener("mouseover", function() {

  element.style.backgroundColor = "yellow";

});
```

- ***Event Object:*** The event handler receives an event object that provides information about the event, such as which element was clicked or the position of the mouse.

```
element.addEventListener("click", function(event) {

  console.log(event.target); // Logs the element that was clicked

});
```

Example of DOM Manipulation and Event Handling Together:

```
let button = document.getElementById("myButton");

button.addEventListener("click", function() {
```

```
  let newDiv = document.createElement("div");
  newDiv.innerHTML = "Hello, I am a new div!";
  document.body.appendChild(newDiv);
});
```

In this example, when the button is clicked, a new div element is created and added to the DOM with the specified content.

4.2.2 What Is the Difference Between innerHTML and textContent?

• innerHTML is used to get or set the HTML content of an element, which means it can include HTML tags, elements, and other markup. For example, if an element contains <strong>Hello</strong>, using innerHTML would return the entire string, including the <strong> tag.

• textContent, on the other hand, only gets or sets the text content of an element, excluding any HTML tags. For example, if an element contains <strong>Hello</strong>, using textContent would return just "Hello".

Example:

```
element.innerHTML = "<p>Some HTML content</p>";  // Includes HTML tags
element.textContent = "Some text content";  // Plain text without HTML
          tags
```

4.2.3 How Do You Add an Event Listener to an Element in JavaScript?

• Elements get event listener activation through the addEventListener() method. Events are activated when both the event type and callback function are defined as parameters for this method.

Example:

```
let button = document.getElementById("myButton");
button.addEventListener("click", function() {
  alert("Button clicked!");
});
```

4.2.4 What Is the Purpose of the Event Object in JavaScript?

• The event object provides data regarding the event's source element together with its type and additional properties as determined by the event. The event handler receives this object when a program triggers the event automatically. You can retrieve particular event details from this object, such as mouse position information or which keys triggered the event.

Example:

```
element.addEventListener("click", function(event) {
  console.log(event.target);  // The element that was clicked
  console.log(event.type);    // The type of the event (e.g., "click")
});
```

4.2.5 How Can You Remove an Element from the DOM?

- You can remove an element from the DOM using the remove() method. First, select the element you want to remove, and then call remove() on it.

Example:

```
let element = document.getElementById("myElement");
element.remove();  // Removes the element from the DOM
```

4.2.6 What Is the Role of addEventListener() in Event Handling?

- The DOM element event listening process depends upon the addEventListener() function. The addEventListener() function enables you to determine the specific event type (click or keydown) along with the callback function that will run upon event occurrence. This method proves better than previous onclick systems since it supports various event handlers for one element while maintaining better functional partitioning within code.

Example:

```
element.addEventListener("mouseover", function() {
  console.log("Mouse is over the element!");
});
```

4.3 Promises

Asynchronous programming is essential within the JavaScript framework since it handles time-consuming tasks such as network requests, file reading, and timers whose completion times remain unpredictable. If operations receive improper management, they will stop other code from executing, thus leading to substandard user experiences. JavaScript runs multiple tasks concurrently when dealing with lengthy operations until they are complete:

- ***Pending*** – The initial state, neither fulfilled nor rejected.
- ***Fulfilled*** – The operation completed successfully.
- ***Rejected*** – The operation failed due to an error.

Promises prove beneficial for asynchronous operations since they give developers a definite method to handle asynchronous code that surpasses callbacks as an older programming approach. You can manage callbacks by utilizing .then() for success results as well as .catch() for error handling instead of embedding callbacks within each other. Promises provide comparative capabilities for easier maintenance of code that improves its readability.

4.3.1 Chaining Promises

Async operation sequences are possible through Promise chaining. The .then() method enables recovery of additional promises that let moving from one sequential execution step to the next. The root cause of callback hell and complex code maintenance can be eliminated with this solution.

Your API call handles data retrieval, after which the received data allows the DOM update or initiates a subsequent operation. The .catch() method works to manage errors from operations when they occur so these mistakes do not interfere with the overall sequence execution.

Async/Await

The ES8 specification added async/await as a user-friendly way to handle asynchronous functions in 2017. The syntax enables developers to write asynchronous code while keeping it structurally and functionally identical to synchronous code for better understanding and debugging purposes.

Async functions produce Promises that get returned from their execution without delay. Inside the function, you can apply the await keyword for halting program execution until any Promise becomes resolved before proceeding to the following statement. Asynchronous code structures appear similar to standard procedural structures through this method, which simplifies code complexity and improves readability.

Async Functions

The definition of an async function results in an automatic return of a Promise. A Promise will get automatically transformed into a resolved Promise and return as the function's outcome regardless of specific Promise return statements. A defined async function enables await usage inside the function while suspension of execution occurs until the promised resolution.

Async functions deliver exceptional assistance for operating multiple asynchronous operations sequentially. Using the await operator lets a function stop running while it waits for a promise to finish before moving to the following code statement.

Awaiting Promises

The await keyword can only be used inside an async function. It pauses the function's execution and waits for the promise to resolve before moving on to the next operation. This provides a more linear flow to your code, making it easier to understand and maintain. It avoids the nesting or chaining of multiple .then() statements, and it also simplifies error handling with try/catch blocks.

Error Handling in Async/Await

The try/catch block provides an effective method to manage errors in async/await programming. A rejected awaited promise will trigger an error that the catch block can receive to handle. The way this method handles errors proves superior to traditional promise chain management because it keeps operations clean and simple to understand.

The sync features of async/await enable direct error catchment in contrast to promises, which require using .catch(). The error-handling system produces cleaner structures useful for handling errors within numerous asynchronous operations.

Benefits of Async/Await Over Promises

Async/await features an even more readable synchronous syntax for asynchronous programming, which outperforms traditional promises regarding asynchronous operations management. Using async/await removes the need for chaining and enhances the readability of code, especially while working with sophisticated asynchronous task sequences. The try/catch block becomes simpler to utilize for error handling because async/await allows developers to enclose all asynchronous operations in a single block.

Additionally, async/await allows for better debugging. When a function uses await, you can step through each awaited operation one at a time, making it easier to isolate and fix issues.

4.3.2 Handling Multiple Asynchronous Operations

Working with multiple asynchronous operations demands a solution to wait simultaneously for all promises to reach resolution. Promise.all() serves this situation by waiting for all promises to finish before proceeding. This functionality helps users execute multiple simultaneous asynchronous operations that need to be done in parallel.

You can also use Promise.race() if you want to proceed with the first resolved promise. This approach is particularly useful when you only care about the first successful result or the first operation to complete.

4.4 Working with APIs: Fetch and Axios

Working with APIs (Application Programming Interfaces) is essential for interacting with external data sources, such as fetching information from a server, sending data to a server, or integrating third-party services into your application. Two of the most popular tools for working with APIs in JavaScript are Fetch and Axios, both of which allow developers to make HTTP requests.

4.4.1 Fetch API

The Fetch API functions as an intrinsic browser tool that enables HTTP request functionality. It is based on promises, making it a cleaner and more modern alternative to the older XMLHttpRequest method. With fetch(), you can request resources from the server, send data, and handle responses using promise chains (.then() and .catch()). Fetch is relatively simple to use and works well for basic API interactions.

The native support of Fetch in current browser versions eliminates the need to install extra libraries. It provides a great degree of flexibility for handling different HTTP methods, headers, and response formats (like JSON, text, etc.). However, the Fetch API does not reject HTTP errors automatically; a promise returned by fetch() resolves even for 404 and 500 error responses. You need to explicitly check for the response status and handle errors manually.

4.4.2 Axios

The third-party library Axios offers popular HTTP request functionality as an alternative solution to Fetch API functionality. The extra features and capabilities of Axios surpass those of Fetch since it performs automatic data response transformations and JSON handling and offers request cancellation functionality. Both request and response interceptors are available in Axios through built-in functionality that enables you to modify requests and responses before they move to your application code.

One of the significant benefits of Axios is its ability to automatically reject promises for HTTP error responses (status codes 400 and above), which simplifies error handling. Axios also has better support for older browsers and additional features like request timeouts, which Fetch lacks by default. While Fetch can be used with more flexibility, Axios's built-in features make it easier to use for complex requests and improve overall development speed.

4.4.3 Request Types

The HTTP request types that Fetch and Axios support encompass GET, POST, PUT, DELETE, and PATCH. These methods correspond to operations on data: retrieving data (GET), creating new resources (POST), updating existing resources (PUT/PATCH), and deleting resources (DELETE). Both tools allow you to set headers, send payloads, and configure request parameters.

While Fetch is more minimalistic, Axios provides additional functionality for handling requests with more complexity, such as including query parameters directly in the URL, adding headers, or encoding request bodies (for example, sending data as JSON). Axios makes it easier to handle scenarios that require advanced configurations like authentication tokens or custom headers for cross-origin requests.

4.4.4 Handling Responses

Once you've made an HTTP request using either Fetch or Axios, the response can be handled asynchronously. Both tools use promises to represent the eventual result of the request. In the case of Fetch, you need to explicitly convert the response to a desired format, such as JSON or text, by calling methods like .json() or .text() on the response object. Axios, on the other hand, automatically parses JSON responses and provides the parsed data directly.

Developers gain greater manipulation capability of response data through Axios' response interceptors and the capacity to intercept responses globally in their application. DevOps can achieve tasks involving response modification between environments or error management through Axios's response interception feature.

4.4.5 Error Handling

Error handling is a critical aspect of working with APIs. When working with Fetch, you need to manually check for HTTP status codes to determine if the request was successful. Fetch will resolve the promise even if the response status is an error (such as 404 or 500), so you need to check the response.ok or response.status properties to verify success.

With Axios, error handling is more straightforward. Axios automatically rejects the promise if the HTTP status code is 400 or higher, and the error is caught in the .catch() block. This behavior is particularly useful when you don't want to manually check for status codes and want to handle errors in a centralized manner.

4.4.6 Supporting Older Browsers

One significant advantage of using Axios over Fetch is its support for older browsers. While Fetch is widely supported in modern browsers, it is not available in Internet Explorer (IE) or certain older browser versions. Axios, being a third-party library, includes polyfills for older browsers, ensuring compatibility across a wider range of environments.

If you're targeting a broad user base that includes users with outdated browsers, Axios may be a better choice because of its comprehensive support for legacy browsers. However, if your application only needs to support modern browsers, Fetch may be sufficient and comes without the need to install an external library.

4.4.7 Promise-Based API

The asynchronous nature of Fetch and Axios makes them promise-based APIs, allowing them to execute operations without stopping execution in the rest of the application. The promise design enables clean management of asynchronous operations and makes failure and success methods easy to use. The promise from Fetch ends in a response object, yet Axios's promise ends with response data, which contains server data.

Although Fetch requires you to manually handle response parsing (like JSON), Axios simplifies this by automatically parsing the response data for you, reducing boilerplate code.

The JSON mode provides valuable assistance for dealing with APIs that deliver JSON data on a regular basis.

4.4.8 Request Configuration

Both Fetch and Axios offer flexible configuration options for making HTTP requests. With Fetch, you can pass an options object containing properties like method, headers, body, and more. This allows you to fine-tune your requests to match the specific needs of the API you're working with.

Axios also allows for extensive configuration, including setting default headers, timeouts, and response types. Axios provides a centralized way to configure defaults, so you don't have to repeatedly specify headers or base URLs for each request. This can significantly reduce code repetition when working with APIs that require consistent headers or authentication.

4.4.9 Canceling Requests

Sometimes, you may need to cancel a request, particularly when working with time-sensitive or user-driven actions. Axios includes a built-in mechanism for canceling requests using cancel tokens, which can be triggered before a request completes. This feature is helpful in scenarios like preventing outdated requests from executing after the user has navigated to another part of the application.

Fetch does not have built-in support for canceling requests, but this functionality can be achieved by using AbortController, a browser feature that works with Fetch to signal a request to be aborted. While this works well in modern environments, it requires more manual setup compared to Axios's out-of-the-box solution.

In summary, both Fetch and Axios are powerful tools for making HTTP requests and interacting with APIs in JavaScript, each with its own strengths. Fetch is natively supported in most browsers and is great for simpler tasks, while Axios provides additional features like automatic JSON parsing, error handling, and support for older browsers, making it a more feature-rich option for complex API interactions.

4.5 Error Handling and Debugging Techniques

Reliable, maintainable code requires error handling and debugging processes to become effective. With its suite of diagnostic tools, JavaScript enables developers to handle errors, which aids them in pinpointing problems successfully while enhancing application performance. Effective error handling helps prevent your application from crashing and provides useful feedback for both developers and users. Debugging, on the other hand, focuses on finding and fixing bugs during development.

4.5.1 Error Handling in JavaScript

JavaScript divides errors into syntax errors which appear from incorrect code structure such as parenexpiration and runtime errors that occur during execution when trying to invoke undefined functions or target nonexistent properties. A user experience needs proper error management for all types of syntax errors and runtime errors.

The try-catch statement represents the fundamental mechanism for error management within JavaScript programs. The code that poses a risk of generating an error exists inside the try block, and the catch block collects any such errors when they happen. Finally, it enables you to run specific code after the try-catch block even when an error does or does not occur.

```
try {
  // Code that might throw an error
} catch (error) {
  // Code to handle the error
  console.log(error.message);
} finally {
  // Code to run after try or catch, such as cleanup tasks
}
```

Error Objects: JavaScript errors are typically represented as Error objects, which contain useful information like a message describing the error, the system displays the file location of the error occurrence, and the line number where the fault occurred. To generate custom errors, users need to use the throw keyword, providing more specific feedback in case something goes wrong in your application.

```
throw new Error("Custom error message");
```

Custom Error Handling: You can develop specific error classes that expand from built-in error classes to enhance your error handling methods. Your application can manage various types of errors precisely by extending the built-in Error class.

```
class ValidationError extends Error {
  constructor(message) {
    super(message);
    this.name = "ValidationError";
  }
}
```

4.5.2 Debugging Techniques

Code debugging involves tracking down code defects to solve them. JavaScript contains multiple tools alongside debugging techniques, which enable you to quickly detect and solve programming problems.

The common practice of debugging code involves using console.log because it enables developers to sled their programs. Manually inserted console.log statements help developers view data values and follow program executions while confirming program functionality. The debugging technique of using console.log generates excessive console clutter, so developers should delete all instances of console.log after finishing their debugging work.

```
console.log("Current value:", value);
```

Breakpoints and Debuggers: For more advanced debugging, you can use browser developer tools, which provide features like breakpoints. To monitor the execution of code, add a breakpoint through developer tools that allows you to stop the program at any selected line and review all important program data. The function enables you to examine each line of your coding sequence until you identify the precise location of errors.

Source Maps: If you are using tools like TypeScript or minifying your JavaScript code for production, source maps allow you to debug the original source code even after it's been transpiled or compressed. Source maps map the transformed code back to the original code so you can debug it as if it were never modified.

A stack trace appears when errors arise in JavaScript because it shows the file sequence that resulted in the error. Error detection becomes easier because a stack trace reveals both when and how the error occurred during program execution. Developers commonly find error sources within browser developer tools, which automatically generate stack traces through the console interface.

4.5.3 Handling Asynchronous Errors

Asynchronous code (such as Promises and async/await) can introduce complexities when it comes to error handling. Unlike synchronous code, errors in asynchronous code can occur at unpredictable times. Handling these errors effectively is essential for building robust applications.

Using .catch() with Promises: When working with Promises, the .catch() method allows you to handle errors that occur during asynchronous operations. This ensures that any errors in the promise chain are properly managed.

```
someAsyncFunction()
.then(result => console.log(result))
.catch(error => console.log("Error occurred:", error));
```

A try-catch block enables error handling when working with async/await. With this method, asynchronous error handling becomes equivalent to synchronous error handling, thus enabling you to handle errors more easily and readably.

```
async function fetchData() {
try {
const response = await fetch("api/endpoint");
const data = await response.json();
console.log(data);
} catch (error) {
console.log("Error occurred:", error);
}
}
```

4.5.4 Error Logging and Monitoring

Developing a system for tracking and managing errors during production is critical because it provides essential user impact information. Sentry, alongside LogRocket and New Relic, serves as an error tracking tool that automatically logs bugs while delivering comprehensive data about their source events. These tools often offer features like user session tracking, stack traces, and notifications when errors occur.

Client-Side Error Logging: You can log errors on the client side using tools like window.onerror to capture global errors or by manually sending error data to a logging service.

```
window.onerror = function(message, source, lineno, colno, error) {

// Send error data to an external logging service console.log("Error
         logged:", message, source, lineno);

};
```

Using Winston or Bunyan in conjunction with server-side error handling enables applications to record and store errors that occur in operational execution for later analysis. The tools enable users to classify system errors by assigning different logging levels, which include info, warn, and error, to prioritize specific issues.

4.5.5 Unit Testing and Test-Driven Development (TDD)

Codes benefit from error prevention through the practice of test writing. The purpose of unit testing is to confirm individual functions and modules function properly, which enables developers to spot errors early before development completion. Developers utilize Mocha as well as Jest for performing tests on their JavaScript code.

Test-driven development stands as an approach that instructs developers to create their tests prior to creating the code. Your code will match specific requirements and function as expected by starting with test writing. The number of identified bugs decreases, and debugging processes become simpler as a result of this method.

4.5.6 Handling User Input and Validation

User-provided information becomes a leading cause of errors, which developers struggle to resolve because they neglect proper input validation steps. Take appropriate measures to authenticate user data entries through client-side and server-side operations to prevent unanticipated system responses and security issues, which could include SQL injection attacks and cross-site scripts.

The form validation component should double-check user contributions before server transmission to validate their accuracy. The application can utilize built-in HTML validation attributes or JavaScript-based validation logic to achieve this security goal.

Always perform server-side validation because client-side validation cannot serve as a standalone method. Server validations should be used to confirm user submissions because such an approach protects your system from dangerous data entry. The validation method implemented on the server also detects situations when users avoid client-side security measures.

4.5.7 Common Debugging Tools

Web browsers come with built-in developer tools that supply users with strong debugging options, including breakpoints as well as console access and network demand and performance display functions.

- ***Linters:*** Tools like ESLint analyze your code for potential issues and enforce coding standards. Using a linter can help catch common mistakes before they become errors in production.

- ***Version Control:*** Through the use of version control systems, including Git, teams can monitor code modifications while you can access previous working versions to resolve coding problems.

Effective error handling and debugging techniques are essential for building stable, reliable applications. By using the right tools and strategies, you can catch issues early, handle errors gracefully, and provide a better experience for both developers and users.

4.6 JavaScript Libraries and Utilities

JavaScript libraries and utilities are pre-written code packages that simplify complex tasks, promote reusability, and improve developer productivity. These libraries provide functionality for handling common challenges like DOM manipulation, making HTTP requests, data manipulation, and even more advanced features like animations and state management. Ready-made solutions available inside JavaScript libraries and utilities enable developers to work more efficiently since they do not need to build everything from scratch.

4.6.1 jQuery

The oldest and most widely used JavaScript library, jQuery, enables users to simplify tasks that include DOM manipulation and event handling as well as animations and AJAX requests. It abstracts away browser inconsistencies and provides a consistent API for working with HTML, CSS, and JavaScript across different browsers. Although modern JavaScript has evolved and many of jQuery's functionalities are now built into the language (e.g., querySelector, fetch()), jQuery is still widely used in legacy applications and can be useful for projects that require fast development with minimal setup.

4.6.2 Lodash

Lodash enables developers to easily manipulate array and object types together with string elements through its collection of utility functions. It simplifies common tasks such as deep cloning objects, debouncing events, performing array operations (e.g., filtering, mapping), and handling more complex data structures. Lodash is a more performance-focused library compared to vanilla JavaScript methods, especially for handling large datasets or optimizing code execution.

Common Lodash functions include _.map(), _.filter(), _.debounce(), and _.cloneDeep(). Lodash's modularity also allows developers to import only the specific functions they need, which can help optimize bundle size.

4.6.3 Axios

The promise-based HTTP client Axios serves as a popular framework to execute asynchronous HTTP requests in addition to processing APIs along with response management. Unlike the native fetch() function, Axios has built-in features like automatic response transformation (e.g., parsing JSON responses) and the ability to handle errors more gracefully by automatically rejecting promises for HTTP status codes 400 or above.

Request and response interceptors within Axios give you the capability to transform requests and responses on a global level. This feature is particularly useful for authentication and error handling. Axios is often favored for its simplicity and ease of use over the native fetch() function, especially when dealing with more complex HTTP requests.

`Moment.js`

Through Moment.js, the JavaScript library performs date and time parsing validation, making alterations and formatting operations. It provides a robust API to handle operations like calculating date differences, adding or subtracting time units, formatting dates into different string formats, and working with time zones.

Although Moment.js has been widely used for years, the library is now considered a legacy project, and the maintainers recommend using alternatives like date-fns or Luxon for new projects. Moment.js continues to be a preferred time library for numerous legacy applications since it offers a complete set of features alongside its user-friendly API.

Date-fns

Date-fns is an alternative to Moment.js that provides lightweight, modern date manipulation utilities. Unlike Moment.js, which is a large library, date-fns is modular and allows you to import only the functions you need, helping to keep your bundle size small. The library includes functions for formatting, parsing, and manipulating dates, as well as working with time zones and durations.

Date-fns is favored for its simplicity and immutability. The functions in date-fns are pure, meaning they do not modify the input date, unlike Moment.js, which can alter the original date object. This makes date-fns more predictable and functional in nature.

D3.js

The web browser utilizes D3.js (Data-Driven Documents), which serves as a strong JavaScript library for building interactive data visualizations with dynamic capabilities. Through D3.js developers can connect data to DOM elements while performing data-based modifications to documents which enables them to create advanced visualization components consisting of graphs and charts and maps and animated visualization features.

D3.js maintains exceptional flexibility because it integrates smoothly with both React and Vue as well as other development libraries when establishing UI components. The learning challenge of D3.js exceeds basic charting tools yet offers superior abilities to process complicated data visualizations on extensive datasets, which positions it as the preferred solution for data visualization work.

Chart.js

A simple and power-packed library called Chart.js enables users to develop responsive, beautiful charts. The main distinction between D3.js and Chart.js emerges from the advanced visualizing control D3.js offers developers, yet Chart.js provides streamlined functionality to generate basic graphical representations of lines, bars, and pies.

With its function of drawing charts through HTML5 <canvas> elements, Chart.js serves applications that need straightforward data visualizations together with interactivity and animations. Due to its user-friendly attributes, developers choose Chart.js as their charting tool when they need to avoid the complicated nature of D3.js.

React

React serves as a JavaScript library that supports the interface construction of single-page applications (SPAs) and their user interfaces. The UI components in React are designed to be reusable while the state management operates efficiently. The virtual DOM structure in React helps optimize page performance by re-rendering only the adjusted sections instead of complete pages.

The JavaScript front-end library React stands as one of the leading choices among developers because it helps them develop interfaces and complex applications. The main responsibility of React lies in view management, yet developers can use libraries including Redux or MobX to handle state management.

Redux

Redux works as a state management tool that pairs with React framework implementations but remains compatible with any JavaScript framework or library. The Redux library enables a single application state storage center for components to interact with state data in a controlled fashion.

The key concepts of Redux include the store (which holds the application state), actions (which describe state changes), and reducers (functions that update the state based on the actions). Redux also helps manage complex state transitions and provides tools like middleware for handling side effects (e.g., asynchronous API requests). While Redux is a powerful tool, it can be overkill for smaller applications, and simpler alternatives like React Context or Recoil may be more appropriate in some cases.

Underscore.js

The utility library Underscore.js functions analogously to Lodash by offering various functions to handle arrays, objects, and functions. Underscore offers standard functions to perform deep cloning and filtering operations together with mapping capability and advanced utility helpers for deep object comparison and template production.

Although Lodash has become more popular in recent years due to its better performance and more extensive feature set, Underscore.js is still a solid choice for simple utility needs. Its smaller footprint and similar functionality make it a viable alternative to Lodash, particularly for projects that prioritize minimalism.

GreenSock Animation Platform (GSAP)

JSlib GSAP functions as a high-performance tool for developing animations through JavaScript. GSAP provides support for tweening while also enabling timeline-based animations and advanced effects, which made it popular among developers for their web application animations, UI elements, and game development.

GSAP offers developers flexible interface features along with fast performance at easy-to-use levels. Through its straightforward API, developers can manage animations and access multiple advanced functions, which allow the creation of complex animations with basic programming commands.

The development process needs JavaScript libraries together with utilities as developer tools because these provide reusable solutions for routine work while improving workflow productivity.

1. Interactive Login Form (with Validation)

```
<!DOCTYPE html>
<html lang="en">
<head>
  <meta charset="UTF-8">
  <title>Login Form</title>
  <style>
```

```
body {
  background-color: #e0f7fa;
  display: flex;
  justify-content: center;
  align-items: center;
  height: 100vh;
  font-family: sans-serif;
}
.login-container {
  background: white;
  padding: 30px;
  border-radius: 10px;
  box-shadow: 0 4px 10px rgba(0,0,0,0.1);
  width: 300px;
}
.login-container h2 {
  text-align: center;
  margin-bottom: 20px;
}
.login-container input[type="text"],
.login-container input[type="password"] {
  width: 100%;
  padding: 10px;
  margin: 8px 0;
  border-radius: 5px;
  border: 1px solid #ccc;
}
.login-container button {
  width: 100%;
  padding: 10px;
  background-color: #0288d1;
  border: none;
  color: white;
  border-radius: 5px;
  font-size: 16px;
```

```
      cursor: pointer;
    }
    .login-container button:hover {
      background-color: #0277bd;
    }
    .error {
      color: red;
      font-size: 14px;
      margin-top: 10px;
      text-align: center;
    }
  </style>
</head>
<body>

<div class="login-container">
  <h2>Login</h2>
  <input type="text" id="username" placeholder="Username" />
  <input type="password" id="password" placeholder="Password" />
  <button onclick="login()">Login</button>
  <div id="error" class="error"></div>
</div>

<script>
  function login() {
    const user = document.getElementById('username').value;
    const pass = document.getElementById('password').value;
    const errorDiv = document.getElementById('error');

    if (user === '' || pass === '') {
      errorDiv.textContent = 'Please fill in all fields.';
    } else if (user === 'admin' && pass === '1234') {
      alert('Login successful!');
      errorDiv.textContent = '';
    } else {
```

```
      errorDiv.textContent = 'Invalid credentials.';
    }
  }
</script>

</body>
</html>
```

2. To-Do List with Add/Delete Feature

```
<!DOCTYPE html>
<html lang="en">
<head>
  <meta charset="UTF-8">
  <title>To-Do List</title>
  <style>
    body {
      font-family: Arial;
      background: #f0f4f8;
      display: flex;
      justify-content: center;
      padding-top: 60px;
    }
    .todo-container {
      background: white;
      padding: 20px;
      width: 300px;
      border-radius: 10px;
      box-shadow: 0 4px 10px rgba(0,0,0,0.1);
    }
    .todo-container h2 {
      margin: 0 0 15px;
    }
    input[type="text"] {
      width: 100%;
      padding: 10px;
```

```
      margin-bottom: 10px;
      border-radius: 5px;
      border: 1px solid #ccc;
    }
    ul {
      list-style: none;
      padding: 0;
    }
    ul li {
      background: #e3f2fd;
      margin: 5px 0;
      padding: 8px 10px;
      border-radius: 4px;
      display: flex;
      justify-content: space-between;
      align-items: center;
    }
    ul li button {
      background: transparent;
      border: none;
      color: red;
      font-size: 16px;
      cursor: pointer;
    }
  </style>
</head>
<body>

<div class="todo-container">
  <h2>My To-Do List</h2>
  <input type="text" id="taskInput" placeholder="New task..." />
  <ul id="taskList">
    <li>Buy groceries <button onclick="removeTask(this)">✖</button></li>
    <li>Finish project <button onclick="removeTask(this)">✖</button></li>
  </ul>
```

```
</div>

<script>
  const taskInput = document.getElementById('taskInput');
  const taskList = document.getElementById('taskList');
  taskInput.addEventListener('keypress', function (e) {
    if (e.key === 'Enter') {
      addTask();
    }
  });
  function addTask() {
    const taskText = taskInput.value.trim();
    if (taskText === '') return;
    const li = document.createElement('li');
    li.innerHTML = `${taskText} <button onclick="removeTask(this)">✖</
          button>`;
    taskList.appendChild(li);
    taskInput.value = '';
  }
  function removeTask(button) {
    button.parentElement.remove();
  }
</script>

</body>
</html>
```

3. Interactive Image Gallery with Modal Viewer

```
<!DOCTYPE html>
<html lang="en">
<head>
  <meta charset="UTF-8">
  <title>Interactive Gallery</title>
  <style>
    body {
```

```
  font-family: Arial;
  margin: 0;
  padding: 20px;
  background: #fafafa;
}
h2 {
  text-align: center;
}
.gallery {
  display: grid;
  grid-template-columns: repeat(auto-fit, minmax(150px, 1fr));
  gap: 15px;
  max-width: 1000px;
  margin: auto;
}
.gallery img {
  width: 100%;
  border-radius: 8px;
  cursor: pointer;
  transition: transform 0.3s ease;
}
.gallery img:hover {
  transform: scale(1.05);
}
/* Modal Styles */
.modal {
  display: none;
  position: fixed;
  z-index: 10;
  left: 0;
  top: 0;
  width: 100%;
  height: 100%;
  background: rgba(0, 0, 0, 0.8);
  justify-content: center;
```

```
      align-items: center;
    }
    .modal img {
      max-width: 80%;
      max-height: 80%;
      border-radius: 10px;
      box-shadow: 0 0 15px #000;
    }
    .modal:active,
    .modal img:active {
      cursor: zoom-out;
    }
  </style>
</head>
<body>

<h2>Image Gallery</h2>
<div class="gallery">
  <img src="https://via.placeholder.com/300/3498db/ffffff" alt="Gallery
        Image">
  <img src="https://via.placeholder.com/300/e74c3c/ffffff" alt="Gallery
        Image">
  <img src="https://via.placeholder.com/300/2ecc71/ffffff" alt="Gallery
        Image">
  <img src="https://via.placeholder.com/300/f39c12/ffffff" alt="Gallery
        Image">
</div>

<div class="modal" id="modal">
  <img id="modalImg" src="" alt="Large View">
</div>

<script>
  const modal = document.getElementById(‘modal’);
  const modalImg = document.getElementById(‘modalImg’);
  document.querySelectorAll(‘.gallery img’).forEach(img => {
    img.addEventListener(‘click’, () => {
```

```
        modal.style.display = 'flex';
        modalImg.src = img.src;
      });
    });
    modal.addEventListener('click', () => {
      modal.style.display = 'none';
    });
</script>

</body>
</html>
```

4. Animated Loading Spinner with Start/Stop Button

```
<!DOCTYPE html>
<html lang="en">
<head>
  <meta charset="UTF-8">
  <title>Spinner Control</title>
  <style>
    body {
      background: #222;
      display: flex;
      flex-direction: column;
      align-items: center;
      justify-content: center;
      height: 100vh;
      font-family: sans-serif;
      color: white;
    }
    .spinner {
      border: 8px solid #f3f3f3;
      border-top: 8px solid #00bcd4;
      border-radius: 50%;
      width: 80px;
      height: 80px;
```

```
      animation: spin 1s linear infinite;
      margin-bottom: 20px;
    }
    .hidden {
      display: none;
    }
    @keyframes spin {
      to { transform: rotate(360deg); }
    }
    button {
      margin: 5px;
      padding: 10px 20px;
      font-size: 16px;
      border: none;
      border-radius: 5px;
      cursor: pointer;
    }
    .start {
      background-color: #00bcd4;
      color: white;
    }
    .stop {
      background-color: #e53935;
      color: white;
    }
  </style>
</head>
<body>

<div class="spinner" id="spinner"></div>
<button class="start" onclick="showSpinner()">Start</button>
<button class="stop" onclick="hideSpinner()">Stop</button>

<script>
  const spinner = document.getElementById('spinner');
```

```
  function hideSpinner() {
    spinner.classList.add('hidden');
  }

  function showSpinner() {
    spinner.classList.remove('hidden');
  }
</script>
</body>
</html>
5. Simple Calculator (Responsive)
<!DOCTYPE html>
<html lang="en">
<head>
  <meta charset="UTF-8">
  <title>Simple Calculator</title>
  <style>
    body {
      background: #f3f4f6;
      display: flex;
      justify-content: center;
      align-items: center;
      height: 100vh;
      font-family: 'Segoe UI', sans-serif;
    }
    .calculator {
      background: white;
      padding: 20px;
      border-radius: 15px;
      box-shadow: 0 5px 15px rgba(0,0,0,0.2);
      width: 260px;
    }
    .display {
      width: 100%;
      height: 60px;
```

```
  font-size: 28px;
  text-align: right;
  padding: 10px;
  margin-bottom: 10px;
  border: none;
  border-radius: 10px;
  background: #eaeaea;
}
.buttons {
  display: grid;
  grid-template-columns: repeat(4, 1fr);
  gap: 10px;
}

button {
  padding: 20px;
  font-size: 18px;
  border: none;
  border-radius: 10px;
  background: #f1f1f1;
  cursor: pointer;
  transition: background 0.2s ease;
}

button:hover {
  background: #dcdcdc;
}

.operator {
  background: #00bcd4;
  color: white;
}

.equal {
  background: #4caf50;
```

```
      color: white;
      grid-column: span 2;
    }

    .clear {
      background: #e53935;
      color: white;
      grid-column: span 2;
    }
  </style>
</head>
<body>

<div class="calculator">
  <input type="text" class="display" id="display" readonly>

  <div class="buttons">
    <button onclick="clearDisplay()" class="clear">C</button>
    <button onclick="appendToDisplay('/')">÷</button>
    <button onclick="appendToDisplay('*')">×</button>

    <button onclick="appendToDisplay('7')">7</button>
    <button onclick="appendToDisplay('8')">8</button>
    <button onclick="appendToDisplay('9')">9</button>
    <button onclick="appendToDisplay('-')" class="operator">-</button>

    <button onclick="appendToDisplay('4')">4</button>
    <button onclick="appendToDisplay('5')">5</button>
    <button onclick="appendToDisplay('6')">6</button>
    <button onclick="appendToDisplay('+')" class="operator">+</button>

    <button onclick="appendToDisplay('1')">1</button>
    <button onclick="appendToDisplay('2')">2</button>
    <button onclick="appendToDisplay('3')">3</button>
```

```
    <button onclick="calculate()" class="equal">=</button>
    <button onclick="appendToDisplay('0')">0</button>
    <button onclick="appendToDisplay('.')">.</button>
  </div>
</div>

<script>
  const display = document.getElementById('display');

  function appendToDisplay(value) {
    display.value += value;
  }

  function clearDisplay() {
    display.value = '';
  }

  function calculate() {
    try {
      display.value = eval(display.value);
    } catch (e) {
      display.value = 'Error';
    }
  }
</script>

</body>
</html>
```

5 Advanced Front-End Frameworks

5.1 Introduction to React.js

The user interface framework React.js functions as a front-end development solution that empowers developers to generate single-page applications (SPAs) that reformat without complete page reloads. Through its Facebook maintenance program, React provides developers tools to create modular components that efficiently handle state data, which enhances application durability. The virtual DOM in React ensures performance optimization by displaying only required interface portions instead of requiring full page rendering.

Figure 5.1 React.js

5.1.1 React Components and State Management

The primary elements of React applications are components, which function as reusable parts that specify how UI elements both seem and operate. The two types of components within React applications are class components and functional components.

The traditional approach to creating React components utilizes ES6 classes within class components. These components allow users to access state values during a component's lifecycle operation.

```
class MyComponent extends React.Component {
  constructor(props) {
```

```
    super(props);
    this.state = { count: 0 };
  }
  render() {
    return <div>Count: {this.state.count}</div>;
  }
}
```

Functional Components: These are simpler components defined as JavaScript functions. Initially, they were stateless; functional components were unable to handle state and side effects until React Hooks arrived and brought this ability to them.

```
const MyComponent = () => {
  const [count, setCount] = useState(0);
  return <div>Count: {count}</div>;
};
```

The ability to maintain and update data resides within components by means of state management in React. The useState hook from React serves to create and manage state instances locally for functional elements while this.state handles the same task for class components. The transition of state in a component triggers React to perform a re-render that leads to a DOM update with the new state values.

5.1.2 React Hooks and Lifecycle Methods

The version 16.8 update of React brought Hooks to allow functional components access to state management capabilities that were restricted to class components only. React Hooks function as methods to let developers access "features" of state and lifecycle components as well as context capabilities.

useState: The use of this hook allows functional components to acquire state functionality. The hook provides a list of two elements, including the current state and an update function.

```
const [count, setCount] = useState(0);
```

useEffect: Function components can run side effects through the useEffect hook, which enables data fetching and subscriptions or manual DOM modification. Function components can achieve the functionality of componentDidMount, componentDidUpdate and componentWillUnmount through the useEffect hook.

```
useEffect(() => {
  // Runs when component mounts or updates
  fetchData();
}, [dependencies]); // Dependency array (runs when dependencies change)
```

React enables developers to implement lifecycle methods within class components for running code during particular points during component lifecycle phases, including both mounting and updating stages.

5.1.3 Routing with React Router

SPAs rely heavily on routing mechanisms to switch between different views or pages without forced page reloads. The React community's standard tool for application routing in React projects is called React Router. React Router provides developers a way to create different routes (URLs) that connect directly to individual components, thus delivering a seamless user interface.

Basic Setup: React Router provides several components like BrowserRouter, Route, Switch, and Link to enable navigation within the application.

```
import { BrowserRouter as Router, Route, Link } from 'react-router-dom';
const App = () => {
  return (
    <Router>
      <nav>
        <Link to="/home">Home</Link>
        <Link to="/about">About</Link>
      </nav>
      <Switch>
        <Route path="/home" component={Home} />
        <Route path="/about" component={About} />
      </Switch>
    </Router>
  );
};
```

Dynamic Routing: React Router also supports dynamic routing, where the content can change based on parameters in the URL. For example, you can create a route for a blog post by passing an id as a parameter.

```
<Route path="/post/:id" component={PostDetail} />
```

Inside the component, you can access the id parameter using useParams() from React Router:

```
const { id } = useParams();
```

React Router also allows for nested routes, redirects, and route guards, enabling complex and flexible routing configurations for large-scale applications.

Developers achieved web application development transformation through React.js because it delivered components with built-in state control systems. Through hooks, React simplified the process of handling state together with side effects within functional components. Navigation through single-page applications gets easy with the use of React Router, and methods from the lifecycle let developers handle side effects and interact with the DOM in a performant way. Modern web development favors React because its flexible framework, modular approach, and high-speed virtual DOM implementation combined create an optimal solution.

5.2 Introduction to Angular

Angular represents one of the popular open-source web application frameworks that Google originally developed. Angular offers developers a development solution through TypeScript that creates complex single-page applications (SPAs) through its extensive set of tools and features structure. Dynamic web applications become easy to develop because Angular offers developers an extensive set of features, including components, directives, dependency injection, two-way data binding, and routing, together with many more.

As a complete framework, Angular offers developers all the necessary tools to construct applications that scale while remaining easy to maintain because it contains router functionality with form-handling capabilities, an HTTP client, and testing capabilities. The fundamental idea of Angular focuses on delivering a component-based structure that supports customizable parts and optimized data organization systems.

Table 5.1 Angular key concepts and features

Topic	Description	Example	Usage
What is Angular?	A TypeScript-based framework for web applications	import { Component } from '@angular/core';	Building SPAs and dynamic apps
Component-Based Architecture	UI is divided into reusable components	@Component({ selector: 'app-header' })	Organizing the UI efficiently
Two-Way Data Binding	Synchronizes data between the model and the view	[(ngModel)]="userInput"	Live updates between UI and logic
Directives	Extend HTML with custom behavior	*ngFor, *ngIf	Looping, conditionals in templates
Dependency Injection	Inject services into components for reuse	constructor(private service: DataService)	Improves modularity
Routing	Enables navigation between views	RouterModule.forRoot(routes)	Single-page navigation
Services	Share logic/data between components	@Injectable({ providedIn: 'root' })	Manages API calls, shared logic
Angular CLI	Command-line tool for Angular project management	ng new my-app, ng serve	Eases development workflow
Performance Optimization	Uses lazy loading, AOT compilation for speed	loadChildren: () => import(...)	Improves app performance

5.2.1 Angular Components and Directives

The core foundation of Angular consists of components along with directives. The view of your application derives from components, yet directives enable you to alter and customize regular HTML elements.

The UI part of an application receives control from components that exist as TypeScript classes in Angular development. Every part of Angular components includes three fundamental elements:

Template: Defines the HTML structure of the view.

• ***Class:*** Contains the logic for the component, including properties and methods.

• ***Metadata:*** Provided via the @Component decorator, it defines how the component should behave and interact with the Angular framework.

For example:

```
@Component({
  selector: 'app-hello-world',
  template: '<h1>Hello, {{ name }}!</h1>',
})
export class HelloWorldComponent {
  name: string = 'Angular';
}
```

The component shows a greeting message that relies on the name property.

• Classes known as directives enable DOM element behavior modification in Angular. Angular includes three main directive categories that affect DOM elements at various levels.

• Structural Directives: Modify the structure of the DOM (e.g., *ngIf, *ngFor).

• Neatly transform your elements through ngClass while ngStyle makes them look attractive.

• Users can design and develop their own directives to wrap particular application behaviors.

Example of using *ngIf directive to conditionally render content:

```
<div *ngIf="isLoggedIn">Welcome, user!</div>
```

In this case, the content is rendered only if the isLoggedIn property is true.

5.2.2 Dependency Injection and Services

Dependency injection (DI) represents a fundamental Angular feature that lets you design object (or service) creation and service dependency management across components and other services. Through loose coupling, DI allows developers to handle dependencies, thus enabling better testing and state management across the application.

Services in Angular are used to encapsulate business logic, data manipulation, or HTTP communication. They are typically injected into components, other services, or directives to provide functionality.

Example of a simple service in Angular:

```
@Injectable({
  providedIn: 'root',
})
export class UserService {
  getUserData(): Observable<User> {
    return this.http.get<User>('https://api.example.com/user');
  }
}
```

In this example, the UserService retrieves user data from an API. The @Injectable decorator marks the class as available for dependency injection, and providedIn: 'root' ensures the service is available throughout the entire application.

Injecting Services: Services can be injected into components using the constructor:

```
@Component({
  selector: 'app-user-profile',
  template: '<p>{{ user.name }}</p>',
})
export class UserProfileComponent {
  user: User;
  constructor(private userService: UserService) {
  this.userService.getUserData().subscribe((data) => {
      this.user = data;
    });
  }
}
```

During this example, the UserProfileComponent constructor receives an instance of UserService. The fetched user data from the service automatically populates the user property before display in the template.

Angular serves as a full-featured development framework that enables simple development of large-scale web applications that are easy to maintain. Dependency injection within the framework helps businesses properly handle their services and business rules, and two-way data binding enables automatic model and view synchronization. Enterprise-level applications become better candidates for development through Angular because of its combination of features and extensive tool package.

5.3 Comparison of React, Angular, and Vue.js

Web applications benefit from the usage of three major JavaScript frameworks and libraries that include React, Angular, and Vue.js. All three frameworks enable developers to build dynamic interfaces, but they have different approaches regarding architecture and learning difficulties as well as flexibility alongside their ecosystems. A comparison between React, Angular, and Vue.js is presented through an analysis of multiple vital dimensions:

5.3.1 Architecture and Design Philosophy

React exists as a user interface development library that functions without complete framework capabilities. The framework implements a component-based architecture that divides the UI into small components that users may reuse. The view layer of React operates through a virtual DOM to achieve performance optimizations across its operations.

Angular functions as an extensive framework that implements Model-View-Controller (MVC) or Model-View-ViewModel (MVVM) architectural models. The framework includes various essential tools for developers that incorporate routing alongside form handling and HTTP client and routing features. Angular implements an opinionated approach because it enforces specific ways to handle tasks, which presents advantages and limitations that adapt to different application needs.

Vue.js functions as a progressive framework bearing structural similarities to React since it adopts a component-based structure. Vue delivers more pre-built features to developers without requiring additional packages since it comes equipped with Vue Router and Vuex for routing and state management features. Vue enables developers to add it to current projects in small steps because it provides incremental adoption as a feature.

5.3.2 Learning Curve

• ***React:*** React has a relatively low learning curve if you're familiar with JavaScript. However, React's ecosystem is vast, and developers often need to learn additional libraries for state management (e.g., Redux) and routing (e.g., React Router), which can increase the learning curve.

• ***Angular:*** Angular has a steep learning curve due to its complex setup and reliance on TypeScript, decorators, dependency injection, and other advanced concepts. Angular's comprehensive tooling means developers need to learn multiple concepts like directives, services, and RxJS (for reactive programming).

• ***Vue.js:*** Vue has a gentler learning curve and is often considered more beginner-friendly than Angular or React. Vue provides a clean, simple API and has excellent documentation, making it easy for developers to get started. Vue can be incrementally integrated into existing projects, so developers can adopt it as needed.

5.3.3 Flexibility and Ecosystem

When using React, developers must select additional development solutions because it provides only view layer capabilities without supplying routing or state management functionality.

Angular supplies developers with the most essential application functionality because its full-stack framework operation includes standard components as defaults. For developers, Angular supplies complete application implementation possibilities since it provides routing alongside form handling, HTTP requests, and other necessary features free from the need for third-party libraries. The structured approach of Angular restricts developer flexibility since developers who need freedom might find it restrictive.

The flexibility of Vue.js is balanced through its features. Because Vue.js provides both a rich framework ecosystem and building blocks such as Vue Router and Vuex, the technology maintains a flexibility that Angular does not offer. According to Vue, developers can utilize built-in scaling tools to expand their applications, but they also have the option to use third-party libraries for additional needs. Developers perceive Vue as an ideal solution because it combines features that strike a balance between the dynamic capabilities of React and complete stack development with Angular.

5.3.4 Performance

React employs its virtual DOM to enhance performance by updating exclusively the sections of the DOM that received modifications. React provides exceptional performance because it optimizes rendering performance through changes in the virtual DOM system so it updates only specific parts. When developers optimize React applications through methods such as code-splitting together with lazy loading, the framework reaches exceptional performance in complex applications.

Angular provides slower performance than React while achieving inferior speed compared to Vue because of its weighty framework along with its two-way data binding feature. Angular contains two performance optimization features called OnPush change detection and trackBy, which allow large applications to work better. Both Angular and Vue need more optimization work to achieve performance excellence; however, Angular demands greater investment than its counterparts, React or Vue.

Vue.js delivers fast performance because it has both a minimal framework core and an efficient reactive system. Its virtual DOM operation works similarly to React, whereas it optimizes the re-render activities. Fast loading times are possible in smaller projects because of Vue's compact structure along with its comparable performance to React.

5.3.5 Community and Ecosystem

The most substantial community base exists for React, along with a broad range of supporting libraries, tools, and resources. The massive community support of React creates security for applications at scale while numerous educational resources and external libraries are available for different requirements.

Angular receives strong community support mainly because of its enterprise application capabilities. Viue.js maintains a bigger community than Angular, but its advanced construct together with opinionated direction reduces its framework ecosystems when compared to React. Angular benefits from complete Google backing and provides its users with detailed documentation support.

The Vue.js community keeps expanding along with its renowned simple and user-friendly codebase. Since its release, Vue has obtained rising popularity among startups as well as Asian developers.

1. Counter App (Using State)

```
import React, { useState } from 'react';

function Counter() {

  const [count, setCount] = useState(0);
```

```
  return (
    <div style={{ textAlign: ‘center’, marginTop: ‘100px’ }}>
      <h1>Counter: {count}</h1>
      <button onClick={() => setCount(count - 1)}> ➖ Decrease</button>
      <button onClick={() => setCount(0)}> 🔄 Reset</button>
      <button onClick={() => setCount(count + 1)}>➕Increase</button>
    </div>
  );
}
export default Counter;
```

2. To-Do List (Add & Remove Items)

```
import React, { useState } from ‘react’;
function TodoList() {
  const [task, setTask] = useState(‘’);
  const [tasks, setTasks] = useState([]);

  const addTask = () => {
    if (task.trim() !== ‘’) {
      setTasks([...tasks, task]);
      setTask(‘’);
    }
  };
  const removeTask = (index) => {
    setTasks(tasks.filter((_, i) => i !== index));
  };
  return (
    <div style={{ padding: ‘20px’ }}>
      <h2>My To-Do List</h2>
      <input
        value={task}
        onChange={(e) => setTask(e.target.value)}
        placeholder=”Enter a task”
      />
      <button onClick={addTask}>Add</button>
```

```
      <ul>
        {tasks.map((t, i) => (
          <li key={i}>
            {t}
            <button onClick={() => removeTask(i)}>✕</button>
          </li>
        ))}
      </ul>
    </div>
  );
}
export default TodoList;
```

3. Live Character Counter

```
import React, { useState } from 'react';
function CharCounter() {
  const [text, setText] = useState('');

  return (
    <div style={{ padding: '20px' }}>
      <h2>Live Character Counter</h2>
      <textarea
        rows="5"
        cols="30"
        placeholder="Type something..."
        value={text}
        onChange={(e) => setText(e.target.value)}
      />
      <p>Character Count: {text.length}</p>
    </div>
  );
}
export default CharCounter;
```

4. Simple Calculator in React

```
import React, { useState } from 'react';
function Calculator() {
  const [expr, setExpr] = useState('');

  const handleClick = (value) => {
    setExpr((prev) => prev + value);
  };
  const calculate = () => {
    try {
      setExpr(eval(expr).toString());
    } catch {
      setExpr('Error');
    }
  };
  const clear = () => setExpr('');
  return (

    <div style={{ width: '220px', margin: 'auto', textAlign: 'center' }}>
      <h2>React Calculator</h2>
      <input value={expr} readOnly />
      <div style={{ display: 'grid', gridTemplateColumns: 'repeat(4,
          1fr)', gap: 5 }}>
        {'123+456-789*0./'.split('').map((val) => (
          <button key={val} onClick={() => handleClick(val)}>{val}</
          button>
        ))}
        <button onClick={clear}>C</button>
        <button onClick={calculate}>=</button>
      </div>
    </div>
  );
}
export default Calculator;
```

5. React Form with Validation

Features:

- *Real-time validation for name, email, and password*
- *Basic checks: required fields, email format, password length*

```
import React, { useState } from 'react';

function SignupForm() {
  const [form, setForm] = useState({ name: '', email: '', password: '' });
  const [errors, setErrors] = useState({});
  const validate = () => {
    const newErrors = {};
    if (!form.name.trim()) newErrors.name = 'Name is required';
    if (!form.email) newErrors.email = 'Email is required';
    else if (!/\S+@\S+\.\S+/.test(form.email)) newErrors.email = 'Invalid email';

    if (!form.password) newErrors.password = 'Password is required';
    else if (form.password.length < 6) newErrors.password = 'Min 6 characters';
    return newErrors;
  };
  const handleChange = (e) => {
    setForm({ ...form, [e.target.name]: e.target.value });
  };
  const handleSubmit = (e) => {
    e.preventDefault();
    const validationErrors = validate();
    setErrors(validationErrors);
    if (Object.keys(validationErrors).length === 0) {
      alert('Form submitted successfully!');
      console.log(form);
      setForm({ name: '', email: '', password: '' }); // reset form
    }
  };
  return (
    <div style={{ maxWidth: '400px', margin: 'auto' }}>
```

```
<h2>Sign Up</h2>
<form onSubmit={handleSubmit} noValidate>
  <div>
    <input
      type="text"
      name="name"
      placeholder="Your name"
      value={form.name}
      onChange={handleChange}
    />
    {errors.name && <p style={{ color: 'red' }}>{errors.name}</p>}
  </div>
  <div>
    <input
      type="email"
      name="email"
      placeholder="Your email"
      value={form.email}
      onChange={handleChange}
    />
    {errors.email && <p style={{ color: 'red' }}>{errors.email}</
    p>}
  </div>
  <div>
    <input
      type="password"
      name="password"
      placeholder="Your password"
      value={form.password}
      onChange={handleChange}
    />
    {errors.password && <p style={{ color: 'red' }}>{errors.
    password}</p>}
  </div>
  <button type="submit" style={{ marginTop: '10px' }}>Submit</
    button>
```

```
      </form>
    </div>
  );
}
export default SignupForm;
```

6 Backend Technologies with Node.js

6.1 Understanding Node.js and Its Architecture

Programmers can execute JavaScript code on a server environment through open-source Node.js technology, which functions across multiple platforms. Before Node.js arrived, developers used JavaScript on client-side web applications, yet this framework enables JavaScript to execute server-side code, thus supporting complete JavaScript application development. Node.js utilizes the Google-developed V8 JavaScript engine to provide features that improve its scalability for network applications.

6.1.1 What is Node.js?

Node.js operates as an execution environment that provides JavaScript code execution abilities on servers. It functions beyond being either a programming language or a framework. The platform utilizes the Google V8 engine as its foundation to transform JavaScript into machine code, thus achieving high performance in server-side operations. Node.js delivers optimal performance for developing programs that need high concurrency and real-time functions such as web servers and APIs.

Node.js utilizes asynchronous event handling through its non-blocking features, which enable it to excellently serve real-time applications as well as APIs along with chat applications because they need to manage numerous simultaneous connections.

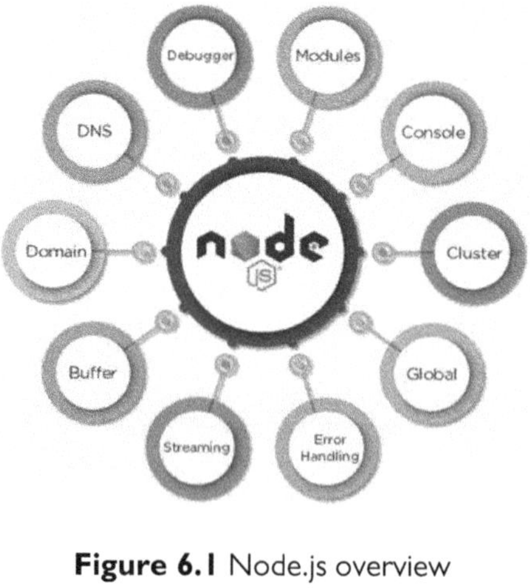

Figure 6.1 Node.js overview

6.1.2 Event-Driven, Non-Blocking Architecture

Node.js makes use of an event-driven, non-blocking I/O execution model as its strongest feature. The procedure of reading files and performing database queries along with making HTTP requests through PHP, Java, and Python serves to block execution flow until each operation finishes. Node.js functions through an event loop and asynchronous operations mode, which prevents blocking from occurring.

Node.js implements an event-based application flow that controls program operations. An event fires a callback function automatically after a task such as reading a file or finishing a database query. Node.js continues processing multiple concurrent requests whenever they arrive because it does not enforce sequential completion patterns before advancing to new requests.

The Node.js platform works asynchronously through non-blocking I/O by performing I/O tasks without blocking the execution process. Node.js proceeds with the next task in the queue before an I/O operation ends, after which it executes the callback function. Node.js accomplishes multiple simultaneous connections efficiently because of its design.

6.1.3 The Event Loop and Callback Functions

Node.js implements its non-blocking I/O model around the event loop component. The event loop manages all asynchronous processes, which allows Node.js to execute multiple parallel operations without obstructing its main operation thread. Node.js implements its event loop function according to the following steps:

Node.js starts by executing the code in a single thread. Asynchronous tasks are added to the event loop queue, which is managed by the event loop itself.

Callback functions are registered for these tasks. When the task finishes (e.g., reading a file, making a network request), the callback is added to the event loop's execution queue.

The event loop processes these callbacks, executing them one by one as the thread becomes available. The event loop component drives Node.js non-blocking I/O implementation processes. By operating through the event loop, all asynchronous processes become manageable, which enables Node.js to execute several parallel operations without slowing down its main operation flow. The event loop function of Node.js follows these steps for execution.

6.1.4 Single-Threaded Model

Node.js uses a single-threaded model for executing JavaScript code. While this might seem like a limitation, it is actually one of the reasons for its high performance. The single thread handles all the application logic, while the non-blocking I/O model allows multiple operations to happen concurrently.

However, Node.js does offload certain tasks (such as file system operations or database queries) to the libuv library, which handles them in separate threads in the background. This way, the main thread remains free to continue executing JavaScript code, while other tasks are processed asynchronously.

6.1.5 Node.js Modules and npm

Node.js has two essential built-in features: the first is its large set of pre-installed modules, and the second is its package management system called npm (Node Package Manager).

Core Modules: Node.js ships with built-in functionality that enables users to execute HTTP requests along with file system operations as well as stream management and path manipulation functions. Through the HTTP module, one creates web servers, while the fs module allows file system interaction.

```
const http = require('http');
const server = http.createServer((req, res) => {
  res.write('Hello, Node.js!');
  res.end();
});
server.listen(3000);
```

npm: The default package manager of Node.js software is named npm. Through npm developers have access to an easy mechanism for both library and module installation and management services. Node.js applications can gain extra functionality through npm by allowing developers to install packages from the npm registry. The express package enables developers to construct web apps and APIs through its use.

```
npm install express
```

6.1.6 Scalability and Performance

Minimal resource utilization exists in Node.js since the programming platform is designed to scale across many concurrent connections. The I/O model, which uses events and non-blocking operations in Node.js, yields great performance for applications that primarily interact with I/O calls. Building CPU-bound applications requires consideration of Node.js limitations apart from its strength for managing multiple simultaneous connections.

Horizontal Scaling: For applications that need to scale across multiple CPUs or servers, Node.js can take advantage of clustering. By spawning multiple Node.js processes, each running on a different core of a multi-core processor, the application can handle a higher volume of requests.

```
const cluster = require('cluster');
const http = require('http');
const numCPUs = require('os').cpus().length;
if (cluster.isMaster) {
  for (let i = 0; i < numCPUs; i++) {
    cluster.fork();
  }
} else {
  http.createServer((req, res) => {
    res.write('Hello from Node.js cluster!');
    res.end();
  }).listen(3000);
}
```

Through the use of a load balancer, production systems can distribute requests into various instances of Node.js applications to use resources effectively and prevent failure points.

Node.js functions as an effective runtime environment that allows JavaScript to execute server-side code. Its event-driven model, which operates without blocking I/O mechanisms together with single-threaded operation, gives Node.js exceptional efficiency when processing simultaneous requests for applications that rely on I/O operations. The scalable architecture, together with strong performance output as well as effortless usage of Node.js, positions it as a superior alternative for real-time functions, APIs, and microservices despite possible limitations with CPU-intensive operations.

6.2 Building a RESTful API with Express.js

Web applications employ RESTful APIs (Representational State Transfer APIs) as a universal standard to send HTTP-based communication requests. Express.js functions as a popular Node.js web framework for building RESTful APIs because it provides fast performance along with minimalist features and flexible scalability. Users can easily create routes and handle requests as well as access databases through this system.

6.2.1 What is Express.js?

Express.js works as an unopinionated lightweight framework that allows developers to create web applications and APIs through Node.js. The framework assists developers by making HTTP request handling more efficient and facilitating the management of middleware systems and REST API creation. Builders can organize applications freely with Express due to its flexible design yet benefit from its key functions like routing capabilities and middleware capabilities.

Table 6.1 Express.js: Overview and key features

Feature	Description	Example
What is Express.js?	A minimal and flexible Node.js web framework	const app = require('express')();
Routing	Handles HTTP requests for different URLs	app.get('/home', (req, res) => res.send('Welcome'))
Middleware	Functions that process requests before response	app.use(express.json())
Template Engines	Renders dynamic HTML pages using templates	app.set('view engine', 'ejs')
REST API Development	Helps build APIs with JSON responses	app.post('/data', (req, res) => res.json(req.body))

6.2.2 Key Features of Express.js for APIs

The API endpoint definition with Express uses a simple yet expressive method for different HTTP actions, including GET, POST, PUT, and DELETE.

The Express middleware system provides developers with functions to address requests while enabling authentication and logging functions before transmitting control to the following functions. Express provides automatic JSON body parsing through built-in mechanisms, which enables easy processing of incoming data. Developers can handle errors through Express due to its intricate error-handling system, which ensures efficient error management.

Integration with databases: Express can connect with databases like MongoDB, PostgreSQL, and MySQL using ORMs such as Mongoose or Sequelize.

6.2.3 RESTful API Structure

A well-structured RESTful API follows common conventions for handling resources. It consists of endpoints that correspond to different actions on resources, usually represented as nouns (e.g., /users, /products). Common HTTP methods used in RESTful APIs include:

- GET: Retrieve data from the server (e.g., get a list of users).
- POST: Create new data (e.g., add a new product).
- PUT: Update existing data (e.g., modify user details).
- DELETE: Remove data from the server (e.g., delete a record).

6.2.4 Setting Up an Express.js API

To build an API with Express.js, developers first need to install Node.js and Express. The setup process typically includes creating an app.js file, initializing an Express instance, defining routes, and setting up middleware for handling requests and responses.

Middleware functions, such as express.json(), are used to parse incoming JSON data, while other middleware (e.g., CORS, authentication) can be added to enhance security and functionality.

6.2.5 Creating Routes and Handling Requests

With Express, developers have access to a mechanism that lets them establish routes between different API endpoints. API routes include an HTTP method along with a URL path along with a callback function that processes requests and provides responses. A GET method retrieves users from a database, whereas the POST method creates new users in the system.

Routes can be organized in separate files to keep the codebase modular and maintainable. Express provides the Router module to define and manage multiple routes efficiently.

6.2.6 Connecting to a Database

The majority of RESTful APIs perform data storage and retrieval operations with the help of databases. Users can integrate Express.js with MySQL and PostgreSQL relational databases as well as MongoDB and other NoSQL databases.

- ***MongoDB:*** Can be used with Mongoose, an Object Data Modeling (ODM) library for MongoDB.
- ***PostgreSQL/MySQL:*** Can be used with Sequelize, an ORM for relational databases.

Database connections are typically established in a separate configuration file to maintain separation of concerns and improve code organization.

6.2.7 Implementing Authentication and Security

Security is crucial when building RESTful APIs. Express provides multiple ways to implement authentication and security best practices:

- ***JWT (JSON Web Tokens):*** Commonly used for token-based authentication.
- ***OAuth:*** Allows users to authenticate using third-party services like Google or Facebook.
- ***CORS (Cross-Origin Resource Sharing):*** Middleware can be used to manage access from different origins.
- ***Rate Limiting:*** Prevents API abuse by limiting the number of requests a client can make within a given time frame.

6.2.8 Handling Errors and Logging

A well-designed API should have a consistent error-handling mechanism to provide meaningful responses to clients. Express allows developers to define centralized error handlers using middleware functions. Logging tools like Winston or Morgan can also be integrated to track requests and errors for debugging purposes.

6.3 Middleware and Routing in Node.js

Node.js relies heavily on two essential elements called middleware and routing, particularly during Express.js development for web applications and API creation. The request-response process in Node.js applications depends on middleware functions, which serve as intermediary elements that enable developers to change requests while conducting authentication procedures and error handling before sending a client response. The resolution process initiates based on the URL and HTTP method, during which incoming requests receive their assigned route.

All middleware execution happens in the defined sequence of application order. These functions operate sequentially within applications to handle operations that include request body parsing, request logging, authentication enforcement, and error management. Express provides built-in middleware like express.json() for JSON parsing and express.static() for serving static files, but developers can also create custom middleware to handle specific functionalities.

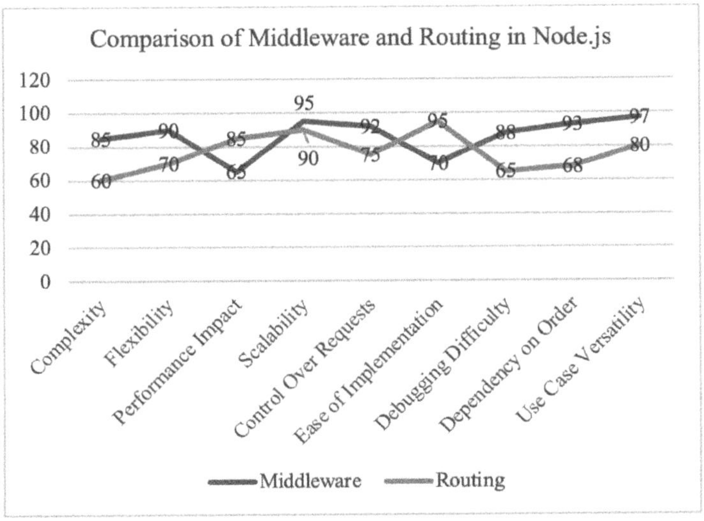

Figure 6.2 Comparison of Middleware and Routing in Node.js

The middleware function accepts three inputs, which include req (request), res (response), and next. Express needs the next function for progressing to the subsequent middleware and route handler. A request will remain suspended indefinitely when the call to next() is omitted. Middlewares operate either across the entire application through global application or only within selective routes based on individual application needs.

Node.js routing through Express provides developers with a system to establish how their applications answer varying HTTP demands. HTTP methods GET, POST, PUT, and DELETE serve as route definitions that represent different CRUD operations. The endpoint /users enables users to retrieve a list through a GET method but allows the POST method to add new users.

Express enables route handling through its Router module, which allows developers to organize routes in separate files for better code maintainability. This modular approach is beneficial for large applications where multiple endpoints need to be managed efficiently. By using express.Router(), different sections of an application can have their own routing logic, making the code more readable and scalable.

Middleware and routing work together to create a structured and efficient request-handling process. Users can reach particular endpoints only after authentication middleware enforces protected route checks. Similarly, error-handling middleware can catch and manage errors, preventing unexpected crashes and providing meaningful error messages to clients.

Error-handling middleware in Express follows a specific format with four parameters: (err, req, res, next). This function is used to capture errors that occur in the application, log them, and send an appropriate response to the client. By centralizing error handling, developers can ensure that all errors are managed consistently across the application.

Middleware can also be used for logging and monitoring. Tools like Morgan allow developers to track incoming requests, their status codes, and response times. This data is valuable for debugging and optimizing performance. Additionally, middleware can be employed to set security headers, enforce rate limiting, and prevent cross-site scripting (XSS) attacks.

Routing parameters and query strings are commonly used in Express to make routes dynamic. Route parameters (/users/:id) allow developers to capture values from the URL, while query strings (/search?name=John) provide a way to pass additional data. Express makes it easy to extract and use these values within route handlers.

When developing web applications with Node.js and Express, middleware plays a crucial role together with routing. Companies can build safer, maintainable programs through middleware execution for request management alongside authentication procedures and error response functions with logging features. This combination produces applications that execute requests effectively alongside a neat and expandable codebase structure.

6.4 Database Integration (MongoDB/MySQL/PostgreSQL)

A Node.js application needs database integration to execute efficient data storage retrieval and administrative functions. Node.js delivers database integration through its support for both the NoSQL MongoDB database and the relational systems MySQL and PostgreSQL. The selection of an appropriate database should be done according to application needs because each system has unique advantages for different scenarios.

The flexible JSON-like format called BSON allows MongoDB to function as a mainstream NoSQL database. The database lacks predefined schemas because developers can store documents without pre-existing structural requirements, which makes it suitable for highly scalable applications that need dynamic data storage. The combination of MongoDB with Mongoose serves as an Object Data Modeling (ODM) library that enables developers to work with the database through schema validation and query-building features.

Integration = Database System + ORM/Query Layer + Application Logic

Where:

• Database System MongoDB, MySQL, or PostgreSQL

• ORM/Query Layer = Mongoose (MongoDB), Sequelize (MySQL/PostgreSQL), TypeORM, or raw SQL queries

• Application Logic Backend framework (Node.js, Django, Spring Boot, etc.) handling queries and data flow

Customers typically use MySQL as their relational database because it organizes information through tables along with rows and columns following a definable schema. A relational database system works best when an application needs complicated issues along with data relationships and transaction processing. The database management system of MySQL operates with SQL (Structured Query Language) to establish, modify, and extract data information. Using the mysql2 package in Node.js, developers maintain direct database connectivity with MySQL servers alongside query execution and data management features.

A Node.js application with an integrated database enhances data handling capabilities through efficient management solutions that offer scalability and maintain program security. The selection of MongoDB for document storage pairs well with MySQL for relational data and PostgreSQL for advanced queries to build a robust application with high performance if developers use the correct best practices for their selected database.

6.5 Authentication and Security in Node.js

The security and authentication measures of Node.js applications serve two important purposes: defend user data from damage and block external unauthorized users. The implementation of secure authentication mechanisms together with best security practices protects applications from potential threats, which include data breaches and both injection attacks and unauthorized access.

Through authentication systems, developers verify user identity before allowing authorization to decide their system permissions. Node.js applications authenticate users through three major methods, which include JWT (JSON Web Tokens), OAuth, and session-based authentication. The authentication method JWT provides a stateless function by issuing signed tokens to clients following a successful login and requiring these tokens with each request for verification purposes.

The authentication protocol known as OAuth establishes a method for third-party services, including Google, Facebook, and GitHub, to authorize user authentication. OAuth 2.0 and OpenID Connect enable secure login between applications and external identity providers through a mechanism that avoids handling user passwords by applications. Authenticating users through sessions depends on server-stored sessions and application cookies, which provide a method to keep a login active throughout webhook requests.

Security of passwords stands as an essential requirement for all authentication systems. Unencrypted password storage creates a significant threat to system security. The cryptographic hashing process using bcrypt happens before a password enters the database for storage. A proper implementation of this method makes it more challenging for attackers to obtain user credentials when database systems are compromised. Secure password policies become more effective when organizations mandate the use of uppercase along with lowercase letters, numbers, and special characters.

API endpoint and route protection stands as a fundamental security task to stop unauthorized users from entering. To secure protected routes, the express-jwt middleware verifies JWT tokens as a request entry requirement. RBAC implements a role-based access system that gives users only authorized actions through predefined access levels according to their assigned roles.

XSS (Cross-Site Scripting) and CSRF (Cross-Site Request Forgery) attacks form two primary security risks that Node.js systems need to protect against. A compromised user data system occurs when attackers embed malicious scripts into web pages. So the risk is lowered through helmet.js, but it provides safe HTTP headers for implementation. Through CSRF attacks, users end up performing unwanted operations on web applications by mistake. Request origin authentication through CSRF tokens protects applications from unauthorized procedures.

By implementing strong authentication mechanisms and following best security practices, Node.js applications can effectively prevent unauthorized access, protect user data, and mitigate common security threats. Regular security audits, keeping dependencies updated, and following industry-standard security guidelines ensure that applications remain resilient against evolving threats.

6.6 Real-Time Applications with WebSockets

Real-time applications, where data needs to be transmitted instantly between the server and clients, are becoming increasingly common. Examples include live chat apps, gaming platforms, collaborative editing tools, and live notifications. Traditional HTTP requests are not well-suited for these use cases because they rely on a client-server request-response model, which does not support bidirectional communication or low-latency data transfer. WebSockets provide an efficient solution for real-time communication by establishing a persistent, full-duplex connection between the client and the server.

The WebSockets protocol maintains two-directional real-time data communication by establishing a continuous connection between servers and clients through a single endpoint. WebSockets provide continuous clientele services communication using one enduring channel, while HTTP demands new link connections each time for a single request procedure. WebSockets provide perfect real-time applications as they eliminate communication delays produced by multiple HTTP requests in a single connection.

WebSockets are easy to implement in Node.js with Socket.IO and the ws module alongside other libraries. Additional features from Socket.IO improve WebSockets to create scalable real-time applications because it provides features for broadcasting, automatic reconnecting, and message confirmation capabilities. WebSocket connections undergo management through the ws module, which provides developers a basic and low-level library for minimal WebSocket connection functionality.

WebSockets provide fundamental user value because they let data travel from the server to the client and vice versa. The server maintains automatic data delivery capability, which operates independently from client demand for requests. Programmers implement instant message updates in real-time chat applications through WebSockets so users always obtain the latest messages without manual refresh actions. A collaborative application shows changes made by users in real time to everyone connected to the shared workspace through the same document.

WebSocket connections begin with a handshake initiated by the client. Once established, the connection stays open until one of the client or server ends it. The WebSocket protocol is designed to be lightweight, with minimal overhead, which is particularly beneficial for applications that need to transmit small amounts of data frequently, such as notifications or status updates.

In addition to basic communication, WebSockets also support features like message broadcasting. This allows a server to send messages to multiple clients at once, which is ideal for applications where a common event needs to be communicated to many users, such as in multiplayer games or live sports score updates. Socket.IO simplifies broadcasting by offering rooms and namespaces, allowing developers to group clients together and send targeted messages to specific sets of users.

WebSockets serve as an effective tool for developing real-time applications using Node.js. The WebSockets protocol maintains uninterrupted messaging between clients and servers, which creates a smooth and quick user experience for messaging tools along with collaborative programs and online games. Proper handling of connection management, scalability, and security ensures that WebSocket-based applications remain responsive, secure, and robust.

7 Cloud Server Hosting

7.1 Introduction to Cloud Computing for Web Development

Cloud computing technology has entirely transformed application development workflows while giving programmers access to large enterprise-level tools. Web development teams can utilize cloud computing to position their websites and web applications on distant servers, whereas before they would need to handle hardware management independently.

The cloud computing domain includes three fundamental service options named Infrastructure as a Service (IaaS), Platform as a Service (PaaS), and Software as a Service (SaaS). Through the internet, cloud computing services present virtual computer resources, including virtual machines and storage, along with networks. Developers can construct and operate applications on PaaS through a platform that eliminates requirements for managing the base infrastructure or application platforms. Through SaaS technology, users gain access to complete functional applications hosted on the cloud by using browser-based access.

Web developers predominantly work with the cloud service models IaaS and PaaS. Through IaaS services including AWS, GCP, and Microsoft Azure, users can deploy web applications by installing virtual machines and receiving both storage and networking resources. The PaaS solutions Heroku and Google App Engine, along with Netlify, deliver simplified infrastructure deployment that enables developers to execute application deployment rapidly.

Table 7.1 Cloud computing in web development: Key aspects

Aspect	Description	Example
Infrastructure as a Service (IaaS)	Provides virtualized computing resources	AWS EC2, Google Compute Engine
Platform as a Service (PaaS)	Offers a platform for application development	Heroku, Google App Engine
Software as a Service (SaaS)	Delivers software over the internet	Google Drive, Dropbox

Cloud computing provides substantial increases in scalability benefits to end users. Service scalability under traditional hosting infrastructure demands manual additions of physical equipment and server enhancements. Applications can protect themselves from increased traffic demand because the system implements automatic adjustments that eliminate both manual worker involvement and application downtime.

Protection stands among the essential items provided by cloud computing systems. Cloud providers enhance their infrastructure security through investments and by providing encryption technology, firewalls, and identity and access management (IAM) features, as well as distributed denial-of-service (DDoS) protection. Administrators of web applications can enable security parameters that developers configure to defend web applications from external threats. Regular backups and disaster recovery tools, which cloud platforms deliver, ensure the applications preserve their resiliency when dealing with data loss or server failures.

Cloud9 and Gitpod serve as cloud-based development environments that let developers create, test, and deploy code in the cloud while minimizing their dependence on physical development systems. These environments come prepared with standard development tools, which enable team collaboration because they work without device setup problems across various devices.

The fundamental components of web development using cloud computing techniques include database and storage solutions. Cloud platforms enable developers to select from various storage options, which include AWS S3 as an example of object storage and Google Cloud Persistent Disks for block storage, alongside Azure Files for file storage systems. Database and large dataset management along with static asset storing ability is provided by these services. Cloud platform users can access managed database services from Amazon RDS, Google Cloud SQL, and Azure SQL Database for automatic administration, including backups and updates and scaling functions.

Cloud computing has a significant effect on the implementation of DevOps practices. Developers benefit from these artifacts that streamline the deployment process by faultlessly delivering new features together with bug fixes to their production systems.

The implementation of serverless architectures becomes possible through cloud computing because it fully eliminates server administration responsibilities. Developer functions within AWS Lambda or Google Cloud Functions perform automatically when triggered by events, including HTTP requests or database modifications. Cloud applications become more affordable through this system because development teams only need to pay for CPU and storage resources actually consumed when their functions execute.

Cloud computing demonstrates excellent capabilities in managing costs, among other benefits. Developers choose from cloud provider payment models where they pay for resources actually used, which lowers infrastructure costs. Cloud platforms provide organizations with different pricing schemes that let them select the most affordable plan that matches their resource consumption patterns.

The adoption of cloud-based development systems allows developers to create and launch web applications through an easier and more performing process. Cloud platforms make developers focused on developing features rather than managing infrastructure through their virtualized resource access and security tools as well as their capability to scale. Cloud operations support full environment control using IaaS solutions, while PaaS offerings provide simple service through web development processes.

7.2 Hosting Platforms Overview: AWS, Google Cloud, Azure, and Heroku

Web application deployment selection determines how your applications grow along with their operational performance levels and financial costs in the cloud environment. AWS/Amazon Web Services, GCP/Google Cloud Platform, and Microsoft Azure, together with Heroku, represent the most widely used hosting platforms currently. Users access specific features and tools through these hosting platforms because they adjust their offerings to match application categories and end-user preferences.

7.2.1 Amazon Web Services (AWS)

AWS has become one of the primary cloud computing platforms, which provides users with a wide array of cloud services, including infrastructure components as well as databases, storage, networking capabilities, machine learning, and analytics features. Within AWS, users access virtual server hosting through EC2 (Elastic Compute Cloud) and object storage through S3 (Simple Storage Service) as well as managed databases through RDS (Relational Database Service). Businesses benefit from AWS scalability along with its pay-as-you-go costs because they only need to pay for what they actually use in their applications that experience varying traffic levels. Enterprise-level deployments find excellent execution within AWS due to its robust security mechanisms alongside its global data center network plus its fully developed automation and DevOps system.

Figure 7.1 Amazon Web Services (AWS)

7.2.2 Google Cloud Platform (GCP)

GCP delivers its cloud services with a concentration on data analytics and networking functions and machine learning capabilities. Through Google Compute Engine and Google Kubernetes Engine (GKE), users can execute virtual machine deployments together with containerized application implementation. The main strong points of Google Cloud include BigQuery's big data analytics capabilities together with TensorFlow's machine learning functionality. GCP maintains an exceptional networking infrastructure that functions exactly like the network systems Google operates to manage its own applications. The platform-as-a-service solution of GCP App Engine enables automatic application scaling, through which developers can deploy applications without managing infrastructure. The system works best with data-intensive applications together with artificial intelligence implementations.

Figure 7.2 Google Cloud Platform (GCP)

7.2.3 Microsoft Azure

Microsoft Azure operates as a comprehensive platform offering enterprise-level solutions and Microsoft product integration. Azure provides its users with various computing services together with storage alternatives, databases, development capabilities, and networking resources. Its Azure Virtual Machines provide IaaS (Infrastructure as a Service) for running virtual servers, while Azure App Service simplifies web app deployment in a managed environment. Azure is particularly appealing to businesses that use Microsoft software like Windows Server, SQL Server, and Active Directory, as it integrates seamlessly with these tools. Additionally, the Kubernetes platform known as Azure Kubernetes Service (AKS) and the CI/CD pipeline infrastructure of Azure enable complex enterprise applications at large scale for businesses.

Figure 7.3 Microsoft Azure

7.2.4 Heroku

Heroku provides easy use and simplicity, which makes it work well for developers who need to speedily deploy web applications without managing infrastructure. Under its role as a platform-as-a-service (PaaS), Heroku enables developers to focus exclusively on code by eliminating server management complexity. Developers can use Heroku through multiple programming languages and frameworks, including Node.js and Ruby, in addition to Python and Java, while accessing numerous add-ons that support database storage and caching functions, logging features, and more. Startup ventures together with small businesses, along with single developers, choose Heroku to rapidly deploy web applications because it provides them with simple deployment without having to handle virtual machine management or networking setup. While it's not as feature-rich or scalable as AWS, GCP, or Azure, its simplicity makes it ideal for rapid prototyping and smaller applications.

Figure 7.4 Heroku

7.2.5 Comparison of Key Features

• ***Scalability:*** AWS, GCP, and Azure offer extensive scalability, allowing developers to manage large, complex applications. Heroku offers scalability but within a more limited scope compared to the others.

• ***Ease of Use:*** Heroku is known for its user-friendly interface and quick setup. AWS, GCP, and Azure are more feature-rich but may require a steeper learning curve, especially for beginners.

• ***Pricing:*** Heroku is often more expensive for larger applications due to its simplicity but is cost-effective for small projects. AWS, GCP, and Azure offer more granular control over pricing, allowing users to optimize costs based on usage, though they may be more complex to set up and manage.

• ***Integration:*** AWS, GCP, and Azure are ideal for complex and enterprise-level applications with high integration needs. Heroku is better suited for developers who prefer a simpler, less integrated solution.

• ***Global Presence:*** AWS, GCP, and Azure have a global presence with multiple data centers, making them suitable for large-scale, globally distributed applications. Heroku's infrastructure is more limited in terms of global availability, which can affect latency for users in different regions.

Each cloud infrastructure targets particular application purposes together with specific development requirements. The powerful infrastructure of AWS best handles enterprise applications that need complex infrastructure systems, yet Google Cloud delivers its best performance for applications that concentrate on data analysis and machine learning. Companies that depend heavily on Microsoft products should choose Microsoft Azure because it provides full compatibility with their current enterprise solutions. The simple approach and learning-friendly operation of Heroku make it an excellent solution for developers who need easy application deployment without complexity for small projects needing consistent rapid development. Selecting the best platform depends on three key factors, such as specific business requirements alongside project size and financial constraints. Developers who grasp these distinct platform capabilities can make appropriate choices.

7.3 Deploying Applications with Docker and Kubernetes

Web development today faces the main obstacle of efficiently deploying applications at reliability requirements and at volumes. Docker, alongside Kubernetes, operates as two vital tools that permanently transformed how developers create packages and send their programs to deployment. The Docker system converts applications into portable containers, which require Kubernetes to automate deployment management for these containerized applications. A combined solution created by Docker and Kubernetes serves to build, deploy, and maintain applications in cloud and on-premise environments.

Through its open-source platform, developers can deploy applications in containers while creating new applications, which they can subsequently run. The standalone executable package known as a container comes with all required elements to execute software applications, which include code together with runtime along with libraries and system tools. Containers maintain separation from one another together with the host system through isolation processes to help applications function identically in any environment. Docker enables easy application development and deployment through its mechanism, which keeps environments consistent across all platforms where containers execute. The consistent framework prevents the frequent software deployment error that software works only on developer networks.

Portability stands as one of the essential features Docker offers to users. Docker enables developers to execute containers through machines that support Docker installation, regardless of whether these machines belong to local development stations, testing facilities, or production servers. The Docker platform enables dependency management alongside maintaining consistent application environments, which generate sameness throughout different development stages, testing periods, and production deployments. Through a Dockerfile, developers define system dependencies with application environment specifications, which they can convert into reusable and shareable images.

After Docker provides its containerization service to a program, a developer can use Kubernetes for further application management. Kubernetes stands as an open-source system for managing container orchestration that enables automatic control of container applications during the deployment cycle and scaling phase and operational runtime. Using Kubernetes, developers gain the ability to handle and implement multiple container deployments throughout their machine clusters. The platform includes functionalities that enable administrators to achieve application availability while maintaining resilience through failures. The basic deployable units in Kubernetes, called pods, get distributed through multiple cluster nodes by Kubernetes so application resources remain optimized while providing high availability.

Kubernetes delivers essential capabilities to control applications throughout numerous machines. The auto-scaling feature present in Kubernetes enables automated application scaling that uses demand-based adjustments of active pod numbers. The application avoids disruptions from peak traffic through an automated adjustment of resources. Self-healing presents an essential automatic function that triggers Kubernetes to replace broken pods so applications stay operational.

The open-source platform allows developers to deploy container-based applications as well as lets them create new applications they can operate. The standalone package called a container includes all software application execution requirements comprising code and runtime elements and libraries and system tools. Isolation processes enable containers to maintain their separate status in regard to host systems and fellow containers for creating dependable application operation across all environments. With Docker, users experience effortless development and deployment of applications because it maintains uniform environments throughout every execution platform for containers. The standardized framework helps prevent the common software deployment issue, which makes software functional exclusively on developer networks.

Among the primary advantages Docker provides to its users is the feature of portability. The Docker system allows developers to run containers across machines that have Docker installation support regardless of the machine type between local development stations and testing facilities and production servers. Through its Docker platform, users can handle system dependencies while upholding uniform application environments, which ensure identical rendering across development phases, then testing phases, then production phases. Developers specify system dependencies together with application environment specifications in Dockerfiles before converting them into shared editable images.

Developers can utilize Kubernetes after Docker provides its containerization service to their programs. The open-source Kubernetes system enables automatic control of container applications through its deployment cycle, scaling phase, and operational runtime. Through Kubernetes, developers obtain capabilities to deploy and manage several containerized applications across their machine clusters. The platform provides specific abilities that enable administrators to achieve application availability while protecting against performance failures. Application resources remain optimized through Kubernetes while providing high availability because the basic Kubernetes units known as pods get spread across multiple cluster nodes.

The Kubernetes system provides control capabilities to manage applications across multiple machines. Kubernetes provides its users with an auto-scaling feature that automatically adjusts active pod numbers based on demand requirements. Peak traffic disruptions are prevented through an automatic resource distribution system in the application. Self-healing represents a critical automated feature that prompts Kubernetes to deploy backup pods for maintaining application uptime.

7.3.1 Benefits of Docker and Kubernetes

• Docker containers provide users with portable solutions that function identically between development testing and production environments.

• Applications utilizing Kubernetes continue operating without interruption since the platform automatically restores and redistributes containers when individual nodes or containers stop functioning.

• The deployment process becomes simpler through Docker and Kubernetes platforms as these technologies automate various operational requirements, which reduces human interaction.

• The automated deployment system of Kubernetes functions through Continuous Integration/ Continuous Deployment to facilitate easy and automated delivery of new production updates.

Application deployment through Docker with Kubernetes management offers a strong solution to handle applications in an efficient and standard manner. Both Docker and Kubernetes enable application developers to produce containers that function throughout all environments and deliver Kubernetes controls for full-scale container management.

7.4 CI/CD Pipelines for Web Applications

The integration of code changes into a shared repository through Continuous Integration ensures automatic testing, which prevents both functional and functional breakdowns. The main purpose of CI is to detect integration issues at the beginning stages of development, which minimizes bug occurrences while maintaining the deployability capabilities of the codebase. Software developers commit their code changes to Git while CI platforms such as Jenkins, Travis CI, or GitHub Actions instantly start running the integration process. The compiling of code happens simultaneously with test unit execution as well as the examination of system defects. Test failures halt the pipeline operation to notify developers about fixing bugs before further processes can resume.

Continuous Deployment serves as an improvement to Continuous Integration by creating an automatic system that deploys tested code directly to production. Through CD, operational deployment occurs without human intervention after a modification passes all of its tests, which results in an automatic transition to the production environment. Through such deployment practices, teams execute new features or implement bug fixes swiftly, which leads to rapid delivery of modified code to end-user systems. The deployment process with CD deploys updates in a consistent manner while maintaining a reliable and efficient operation even if the application increases in complexity.

Web applications need several CI/CD pipeline stages that carry out particular operations for successful integration testing and deployment of code. Here are the main stages that make up a typical automated deployment process:

Integration of code begins when developers submit changes through a version control system that includes Git. The repository system can be hosted by GitHub, Bitbucket, or GitLab.

A build process starts its execution when new code commits appear in the repository. The application moves through various stages during the build process until it completes compilation tasks while bundling assets together for testing purposes. Application dependencies in Node.js web development are installed through npm or yarn, while application compilation or transpilation tasks are executed using Webpack or Babel, respectively.

Automated tests are executed after build completion for checking whether new code has introduced bugs. Popular testing tools for development projects consist of Jest, Mocha, and Cypress. Among the tests are unit tests, integration tests, and end-to-end tests, which belong to this stage. Test failures trigger an automatic pipeline stoppage, which then activates developer notifications about the detected problems.

The application gets sent to the staging environment after passing tests because it contains a production-like setup. Testing in a production-like environment becomes possible through this deployment method because the application operates under real-world conditions. At this stage, application developers, together with employees from quality assurance (QA) teams, conduct manual verification tests to check that the application functions appropriately.

After successful staging testing, the system deploys automatically to the production server. Gaining manual approval stands as the only necessary human involvement in production deployment, with most CI/CD pipelines operating fully automatically. The deployment process through cloud services includes services from AWS, Azure, and Heroku, as well as Docker, along with Kubernetes or similar orchestration tools.

The application goes under real-time monitoring following deployment to check for smooth operation. Every metric regarding performance alongside user activity and errors is tracked by monitoring tools including New Relic, Datadog, or Prometheus. ATIC surfaces alerts that inform both the operations team and the development team about production-related issues, hence enabling immediate issue resolution.

7.4.1 Benefits of CI/CD for Web Applications

The development process and deployment operations reach high speeds through CI/CD systems, which speed up the deployment of new features to production with quick bug fixes and enhancements.

The automated testing system protects existing features from new code-induced failures, which results in higher application quality before deployment.

Automated pipelines guarantee that integration and deployment operate uniformly across development, testing, staging, and production, which eliminates mistakes emanating from involving human factors.

Team deployments of smaller, frequent changes offer better protection because developers can detect problems during initial stages, therefore preventing major bugs from reaching production.

The CI/CD system enhances developer-operations-technical testing team collaboration through automated deployment examination processes, which makes testing quicker and eliminates team conflict.

7.4.2 Common Tools for CI/CD Pipelines

Jenkins functions as the leading open-source automation server for ensuring application building and testing functions and deployment operations. The tool supports plugins that let users connect various development tools and services.

Open-source developers usually choose Travis CI as their cloud-based CI platform. This CI tool functions smoothly with GitHub repositories while it automatically runs build tests together with deployment processes.

CircleCI operates as a cloud-based CI/CD platform that manages development pipelines while linking with GitHub and Bitbucket. The service delivers quick build operations alongside adaptable characteristics.

With GitHub Actions, users can manage full CI/CD functionalities through a native interface from GitHub, which helps them establish automated workflows to create tests and deploy code.

The GitLab CI/CD function within GitLab delivers a total CI/CD pipeline resolution that automates building processes and testing in addition to deployment operations and monitoring activities.

AWS CodePipeline delivers full management for CI/CD services as an AWS solution that automates application deployment on AWS infrastructure.

Modern web development depends on CI/CD pipelines because these systems ensure automated application deployment solutions with consistent and reliable delivery. Achieving faster feature delivery together with superior code quality while promoting great inter-team collaboration becomes possible through the implementation of CI/CD practices. Web applications reach seamless and efficient deployment when organizations use proper tools and processes that reduce both manual errors and technical risks in production deployment.

7.5 Serverless Architecture: Functions-as-a-Service (FaaS)

The rise of serverless architecture has brought widespread popularity through a system that enables developers to develop and launch applications without server management responsibilities. Within serverless computing, one finds Functions-as-a-Service (FaaS), which provides a platform that enables developers to create manageable small functions that execute dependent on events while eliminating the need to operate the infrastructure.

The cloud provider runs the functions through managed servers in a serverless environment while it also provides provisioning and scaling in addition to server management. The misapprehension regarding "serverless" exists because servers execute code, yet developers lack control over server maintenance or management responsibilities. Organizations only need to develop business logic functions that serverless environments execute automatically when users trigger specified events.

7.5.1 Key Features of Functions-as-a-Service (FaaS)

The design of FaaS uses events as triggers to activate functions during automated program execution. The system triggers functions in response to HTTP requests along with database modifications, file transfers, and queue message events. The cloud provider will execute the function upon event triggering.

Automatic scaling stands as a main benefit of serverless functions because they adjust their capacity automatically based on the level of customer demand. A trigger event causes the cloud platform to secure resources for executing the function automatically. Multiple events enable parallel execution of the function's instances in the cloud environment. The system functions differently under low-demand conditions because it performs a scale-down operation that eliminates resource spending and decreases costs.

You only need to pay for the usage of compute resources in FaaS deployment. Functions receive their prices based on two factors: execution duration as well as resource requirements. Such cost benefits become especially crucial for systems having irregular workload patterns because they eliminate expenses for unused server resources.

Serverless architecture allows developers to eliminate complete server management tasks from their responsibilities. Developers can allocate their time to code development and business logic creation because they are freed from managing infrastructure, applying server patches, and performing scalability tasks. The cloud provider manages every aspect of server creation while performing ongoing maintenance along with resource adjustments.

Serverless environments demand functions that function independently from prior executions. Serverless functions exist separately from their earlier executions since each operation runs independently. External services such as object storage or databases serve as a necessary solution to preserve state information when sharing data between function calls.

7.5.2 Common Use Cases for FaaS

Serverless functions provide an optimal solution for creating microservices architectures. The system can activate each function for managing separate business logic domains through single deployment units that function independently for scale and management.

Function As A Service (FaaS) serves as a tool for managing vast amounts of data that occur when specific events take place. When a file upload occurs in a cloud storage service, one function initiates automatic processing, which performs tasks such as image resizing along with video transcoding and log analysis.

The database logic may be implemented using functions to create real-time web applications that execute backend triggers based on user actions or incoming data. For example, a chat application can use serverless functions to process messages or notifications in real time.

API Backend: FaaS can be used to build RESTful APIs or GraphQL endpoints. For example, AWS Lambda or Azure Functions can handle HTTP requests and return responses, serving as the backend for a frontend web or mobile application.

IoT Applications: Serverless functions are suitable for Internet of Things (IoT) applications where devices generate events that trigger processing, such as data ingestion, analytics, or alerts. Functions can handle events from sensors or devices and provide real-time processing.

7.5.3 Popular Serverless Platforms and Providers

AWS Lambda stands as one of the most well-known FaaS products in the market. The service enables developers to execute code through the numerous events triggered by AWS services, including API Gateway for HTTP requests, S3 for file uploads, DynamoDB for database modifications, and numerous additional services.

Users can develop event-driven applications with Google Cloud Functions through its serverless platform. Google Cloud Functions operates for HTTP-triggered functions as well as handling cloud storage events and integrates providers for other Google Cloud services.

The cloud-based computing solution from Microsoft is named Azure Functions. Users can activate Azure Functions through multiple trigger events, including HTTP requests together with storage changes as well as service bus messages, while it provides strong connectivity to other Azure services.

IBM Cloud Functions integrates Apache OpenWhisk to help developers create FaaS functions that respond to diverse events. The service allows developers to use multiple programming languages inside its architecture while connecting to IBM Cloud services.

Cloudflare Workers let developers execute JavaScript code directly from the Cloudflare network's perimeter. The system optimizes fast application performance by running code in closer proximity to end users for low-latency purposes.

7.6 Monitoring and Scaling Web Applications in the Cloud

When web applications expand to serve larger numbers of users, performance together with availability issues must be handled as an essential problem. Web applications receive monitoring together with both automatic scaling and administration capabilities from cloud platforms to keep them functional under changing loads and performant at all times. Team success happens through automated cloud technologies, which enable developers to concentrate on their core work rather than repetitive tasks.

7.6.1 Monitoring Web Applications

Monitoring involves continuously tracking the performance, health, and usage metrics of a web application. It helps detect issues before they affect users and provides insights into how the application behaves in different environments. There are several key areas to monitor in a web application:

Performance Metrics: The way applications perform runs better through the use of performance measurement criteria. The principal performance indicators for observation are server CPU and memory utilization together with response times and database query performance metrics and load times and error rate measurement. Developers determine system bottlenecks through monitoring these performance parameters.

Availability and Uptime: Ensuring that a web application is always available to users is crucial. Cloud platforms offer services to monitor application availability in real time, with alerts sent when issues such as downtime or slow responses are detected. These services often use synthetic monitoring, where they simulate user interactions to test availability from different geographical locations.

Logs: Logs provide detailed insights into what is happening inside the application. They capture system errors, warnings, user activity, and more. Cloud services allow developers to collect, centralize, and analyze logs, making it easier to track down problems and trace application behavior across distributed systems.

Error Tracking: Monitoring error rates is essential for identifying and addressing bugs in the application. Cloud-based error monitoring tools can help developers quickly identify the source of errors, whether they are related to server issues, client-side problems, or database failures. Services like Sentry or New Relic provide real-time error tracking with detailed stack traces and logs.

Real-time monitoring tools with dashboards offer application developers live monitoring capabilities of the current application status. Through dashboards, developers with operations teams can rapidly check the state of their application by viewing vital metric aggregates so they can quickly respond to problems that occur.

Monitoring how users behave while interacting with the application needs significant attention. To enhance user experience, developers need to grasp user paths and points where users leave and identify system obstacles. Google Analytics, along with Mixpanel or Hotjar, provides platforms to monitor user behaviors, which helps identify application improvement zones for better performance together with enhanced user engagement.

7.6.2 Scaling Web Applications

The ability of an application to manage higher loads regarding traffic and data processing falls under the category of scaling. Cloud platforms deliver multiple scale methods that maintain application performance quality under growing demand situations. Organizations have two main approaches for scaling their systems.

When conducting Vertical Scaling we add increased resources including CPU and RAM and storage capacity to one server or instance. The server's individual capacity controls the extent of this scaling method, which suits applications with small to medium traffic volumes. Vertical scalability reaches its limits while being expensive, so developers prefer the more suitable horizontal scaling approach for big applications.

The process of handling higher traffic requires organizations to implement horizontal scaling or scaling out by deploying additional instances or servers. The method proves particularly efficient when implemented with cloud systems since it enables users to set up virtual machines (VMs) or containers upon demand. The system performs automatic horizontal scaling operations depending on traffic volumes to maintain high application responsiveness throughout busy usage periods.

A main feature of cloud computing delivers auto-scaling functionality, which automatically expands applications according to usage requirements. The cloud platform performs self-triggered increases or decreases of instances automatically through metric-based rules such as CPU utilization, request rates, or memory usage.

Segregation of network traffic occurs with load balancing through this method, which distributes traffic across multiple servers to stop one server from becoming overloaded. Cloud providers grant their clients managed load balancer systems that use multiple standards, such as server conditions, alongside performance criteria and physical location data to direct traffic automatically. The AWS Elastic Load Balancer (ELB), among other services, demonstrates automatic healthy instance traffic routing, while Google Cloud Load Balancing also enables this functionality.

Cloud applications implement elasticity as their main feature through their capability to manage resources using up-or-down scale adjustments based on changing demand patterns. Through cloud application elasticity, the system automatically responds to unexpected traffic increases instead of requiring human operators to manage the situation. Resource allocation becomes efficient because additional resources are provided only at the moment of necessity, which saves costs during periods of minimal demand.

Database scaling functions as an essential element for performing cloud application scaling. Automatic resource adjustments are standard functionality for cloud databases, including Amazon RDS, Google Cloud SQL, and Azure SQL Database. Similar databases accommodate large applications through sharding and replication techniques that distribute database content across different platforms or duplicate other databases for additional read operations.

An effective speed improvement comes from implementing caching, which reduces load on backend servers and databases. The frequent data retrieval process becomes faster with cloud services, including Amazon ElastiCache, Google Cloud Memorystore, and Azure Redis Cache, because they enable database caching to reduce server stress.

8 Advanced Topics in Web Development

8.1 Progressive Web Applications (PWAs)

Progressive Web Applications (PWAs) are a new generation of web applications that offer a native app-like experience while maintaining the accessibility and flexibility of a web application. PWAs leverage modern web technologies and best practices to deliver fast, reliable, and engaging user experiences across various platforms, including desktops, tablets, and mobile devices.

PWAs are designed to work seamlessly in any environment—whether the user has an internet connection or not—by utilizing features like offline access, push notifications, and background sync. They can be installed on a device and launched from the home screen, just like native mobile apps, but they are built using standard web technologies such as HTML, CSS, and JavaScript.

8.1.1 Key Features of PWAs

Responsive Design: PWAs are built to work across various devices, ensuring that the app's design adapts to different screen sizes, orientations, and devices. Whether accessed on a phone, tablet, or desktop, PWAs provide a consistent user experience.

Offline Functionality: One of the standout features of PWAs is their ability to work offline or in low-network conditions. This is achieved through service workers, which cache assets and content on the user's device, allowing the app to function even when there is no internet connection.

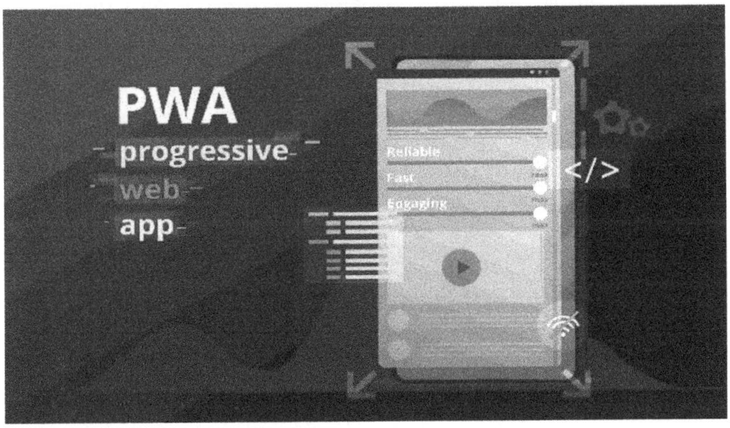

Figure 8.1 PWAs overview

App-Like Experience: PWAs provide an app-like experience through smooth animations, transitions, and a consistent UI. Users can interact with the app just like they would with a native app, including adding it to the home screen, launching it from an icon, and enjoying full-screen mode without a browser's address bar.

Push Notifications: PWAs support push notifications, allowing applications to send updates, reminders, and alerts to users even when the app is not actively open. Push notifications are a key tool for increasing user engagement and retention.

Fast Loading and Performance: PWAs are optimized for performance by using techniques such as lazy loading, efficient caching, and minimal network requests. This results in fast load times, even on slower networks, improving the overall user experience.

Installability: Unlike traditional web apps, PWAs can be "installed" on a user's device. Users can add the app to their home screen directly from the browser, and it will function like a native app, with its own icon and full-screen view. Installation is frictionless and does not require going through an app store.

Security: PWAs are served over HTTPS, ensuring that all data transmitted between the app and the server is secure. This is especially important in protecting user data and maintaining privacy standards.

Background Sync: PWAs can sync data with the server in the background, ensuring that user data is up to date even when the app is not actively being used. This feature is useful for apps that rely on data input or updates, such as messaging apps or news aggregators.

8.1.2 Benefits of PWAs

Cross-Platform Compatibility: Since PWAs are built with web technologies, they can be run on any platform with a modern web browser, making them highly accessible across devices, from Android and iOS to Windows and macOS.

Improved Performance: PWAs are designed to load quickly and provide a seamless user experience, even on slow or unreliable networks, which helps improve user retention and satisfaction.

Reduced Development Costs: PWAs eliminate the need for separate development teams for web, iOS, and Android applications. With a single codebase, developers can deliver an app-like experience across multiple platforms, reducing the overall cost of development and maintenance.

Easy Updates: PWAs are easy to update, as updates are deployed directly to the web server and automatically available to users when they load the app. This avoids the need for users to manually update the app through an app store.

No App Store Approval: PWAs do not require app store approval for distribution. This enables faster deployment and iteration of features without waiting for approval from app store reviewers.

Increased Engagement: With features like push notifications, offline access, and the ability to be installed on the user's device, PWAs help increase user engagement and retention, especially for apps that require frequent interaction.

8.1.3 How PWAs Work

PWAs rely on three core technologies to deliver their functionality:

Service Workers: Service workers are JavaScript files that run in the background and enable features like offline functionality, push notifications, and background sync. They intercept network requests and can serve content from the cache, even when the user is offline.

Web App Manifests: The web app manifest is a JSON file that contains metadata about the app, such as its name, icons, start URL, and display preferences. This allows the web app to be installed on the user's device and behave like a native app.

HTTPS: PWAs must be served over HTTPS to ensure secure communication between the client and server. This guarantees that all data exchanged is encrypted and that the integrity of the app is maintained.

8.1.4 Challenges of PWAs

Limited iOS Support: While PWAs are widely supported on Android and many desktop platforms, iOS has limited support for certain PWA features, such as push notifications. This can restrict the full potential of PWAs for iOS users.

Storage Limitations: PWAs are subject to storage limitations on certain devices, which can affect their ability to store large amounts of data locally, particularly on mobile devices with limited storage.

Discoverability: Since PWAs are accessed through web browsers, they may face challenges in discoverability compared to native apps, which can be promoted through app stores. Developers need to rely on SEO, social media, and marketing efforts to promote their PWAs.

Complexity in Development: While PWAs can be simpler to develop than traditional native apps, integrating features like service workers, caching, and push notifications can still add complexity. Developers need to be familiar with modern web technologies and best practices to ensure the PWA performs well across all devices and networks.

Progressive Web Applications (PWAs) represent a new paradigm in web development, combining the best of web and native app experiences. With features like offline access, push notifications, and installability, PWAs offer a powerful way to engage users across devices without the need for complex native development. While there are some challenges, such as limited support on iOS and storage limitations, the advantages of faster load times, cross-platform compatibility, and cost savings make PWAs an attractive solution for modern web applications. By leveraging the power of PWAs, businesses can reach more users and provide a superior experience, whether online or offline.

8.2 Web Performance Optimization Strategies

Web performance optimization is crucial for ensuring that a website or web application loads quickly, performs well, and provides an excellent user experience. Slow websites can lead to high bounce rates, lower user engagement, and ultimately, a loss in revenue. As web technologies evolve, so do the strategies for improving performance. There are several key strategies and best practices that developers can employ to optimize web performance, focusing on aspects such as loading speed, responsiveness, and overall user experience.

8.2.1 Minimize HTTP Requests

Every resource (like images, scripts, and stylesheets) on a web page requires an HTTP request to be loaded. Reducing the number of HTTP requests can significantly improve loading times. Some techniques to minimize HTTP requests include:

Table 8.1 Minimizing HTTP requests: Best practices

Technique	Description	Example
Combine CSS & JS Files	Reduces multiple requests by merging files	Use a single styles.css and scripts.js
Use Image Sprites	Combines multiple images into one to reduce requests	CSS sprites for icons, buttons
Enable Caching	Stores static resources locally to avoid repeated downloads	Cache-Control & ETag headers
Use Content Delivery Network (CDN)	Distributes assets across global servers for faster loading	Host libraries on a CDN (e.g., jQuery on Cloudflare)
Lazy Loading	Loads images and scripts only when needed	loading="lazy" for images

Combining Files: Combine multiple CSS or JavaScript files into a single file to reduce the number of requests.

Image Sprites: Combine multiple small images into a single image sprite to reduce the number of image requests.

Inlining Small Files: For very small CSS or JavaScript files, consider inlining them directly into the HTML to avoid an extra HTTP request.

8.2.2 Optimize Images

Images are often the largest files on a web page, so optimizing them can have a significant impact on performance. Some image optimization strategies include:

• ***Compression:*** Compress images to reduce file size without losing quality. Tools like ImageOptim, TinyPNG, and WebP (a modern image format) can help achieve this.

• ***Lazy Loading:*** Load images only when they are needed (i.e., when they come into view as the user scrolls down the page). This can reduce initial load time and save bandwidth for users who may not scroll through the entire page.

• ***Responsive Images:*** Serve appropriately sized images based on the user's screen resolution and size, ensuring that users don't download unnecessarily large images.

8.2.3 Leverage Browser Caching

Caching allows frequently used resources to be stored locally in the user's browser, reducing the need for repeated downloads. By setting appropriate cache headers, resources can be cached for a specific time period, ensuring that users don't have to re-download static assets on each visit.

Cache Control: Use Cache-Control headers to specify caching rules for different resources. For example, you can cache images and fonts for a long period, while setting a shorter cache duration for dynamic content like HTML or JavaScript files.

ETags: Use ETags (Entity Tags) to track changes in files and avoid unnecessary re-downloads of unchanged resources.

8.2.4 Prioritize Above-the-Fold Content

Above-the-fold content refers to the portion of the web page that is visible without scrolling. Prioritizing this content ensures that users can start interacting with the page while the rest of the content continues to load.

Lazy Loading: Load resources that are not immediately visible (like images or JavaScript) after the above-the-fold content is fully loaded.

Critical Rendering Path Optimization: Optimize the order in which resources are loaded, ensuring that critical content is loaded first while less important assets are deferred.

8.2.5 Reduce JavaScript and CSS Blocking Time

Rendering performance can be negatively affected by JavaScript and CSS files that block the rendering process. To improve this, consider the following:

Inline Small CSS and JavaScript: For critical inline scripts and styles that are needed immediately, place them directly within the HTML to avoid additional HTTP requests.

Use HTTP/2: HTTP/2 allows multiple requests to be multiplexed over a single connection, reducing latency and improving loading times.

8.2.6 Monitor and Test Performance Regularly

It's essential to continuously monitor the performance of your web application and make adjustments as needed. Use performance testing tools to identify bottlenecks and ensure that your optimizations are working effectively.

Google Lighthouse: Google Lighthouse is a popular open-source tool for auditing performance, accessibility, and SEO. It provides a detailed report of performance metrics and suggests optimizations.

WebPageTest: WebPageTest allows you to test the performance of your website from different locations, devices, and browsers.

Chrome DevTools: Chrome DevTools can be used to analyze load performance, identify slow resources, and debug performance issues.

Web performance optimization is an ongoing process that requires attention to detail and a thorough understanding of how different factors can impact load times and user experience. By reducing HTTP requests, optimizing images, leveraging caching, and using CDNs, developers can significantly improve web performance. Additionally, minifying resources, compressing files, and prioritizing above-the-fold content can lead to faster load times and smoother interactions. Regular monitoring and testing using tools like Google Lighthouse and WebPageTest will ensure that performance remains optimal as the web application evolves. Ultimately, faster web performance leads to better user engagement, higher conversion rates, and improved SEO rankings.

8.3 Search Engine Optimization (SEO) Best Practices

Search Engine Optimization (SEO) is the practice of improving the visibility of a website or web application in search engine results. SEO involves optimizing both the content and the technical aspects of a site to ensure that search engines like Google can easily crawl, index, and understand the content. The goal of SEO is to improve the rankings of a site, which ultimately increases traffic and enhances the user experience.

One of the key components of SEO is keyword research. By identifying the terms and phrases users are searching for, web developers and content creators can tailor their content to match those queries. Integrating relevant keywords naturally into the content ensures that search engines can match the website with the appropriate search queries. However, overstuffing keywords or using them unnaturally can lead to penalties from search engines, so it is important to focus on creating content that is both valuable and relevant to the target audience.

Another important SEO strategy is optimizing the on-page elements of a website, such as title tags, meta descriptions, and headings. Title tags should accurately describe the page content while incorporating important keywords. Meta descriptions, although not directly impacting rankings, serve as a brief summary that appears in search engine results, influencing click-through rates. Using proper heading tags (H1, H2, etc.) not only helps organize content for readers but also helps search engines understand the structure and hierarchy of the page.

Mobile optimization has become an essential factor for SEO, especially with the increasing use of mobile devices to browse the web. Google has adopted mobile-first indexing, meaning that it primarily uses the mobile version of a site to determine its rankings. Therefore, ensuring that a site is responsive and provides a seamless user experience across different screen sizes is crucial for SEO success. This includes optimizing load speeds, improving touch interactivity, and ensuring that content is easily readable on smaller screens.

Page speed is another critical ranking factor for SEO. Websites that load slowly can result in a poor user experience, leading to higher bounce rates and lower engagement. Search engines prioritize fast-loading pages, and improvements such as compressing images, minifying code, and utilizing caching techniques can help enhance site speed. Tools like Google PageSpeed Insights can help developers analyze and optimize the performance of a site to improve both speed and usability.

Finally, monitoring SEO performance through analytics tools is essential to understand how a site is performing and where improvements can be made. Tools like Google Analytics and Google Search Console provide valuable insights into traffic sources, user behavior, and keyword performance. By regularly reviewing these metrics and making data-driven adjustments, webmasters can ensure that their SEO strategies remain effective over time.

SEO is an ongoing process that requires a combination of technical optimization, quality content creation, and user-focused strategies. By focusing on keyword research, on-page elements, mobile optimization, page speed, and acquiring backlinks, web developers can improve a website's search engine rankings. Additionally, regular monitoring and updates are essential to maintain SEO success and adapt to evolving search engine algorithms. SEO best practices help enhance the visibility of a site, driving organic traffic and contributing to its overall success.

8.4 Accessibility in Web Applications

Accessibility in web applications refers to the practice of designing and developing websites in a way that ensures they are usable by all people, including those with disabilities. Web accessibility involves creating content that can be accessed by individuals with visual, auditory, motor, and cognitive impairments, using various assistive technologies like screen readers, voice recognition software, and keyboard navigation. Ensuring accessibility is not only a matter of legal compliance but also a critical factor in providing an inclusive, user-friendly experience for all users.

One of the key principles of web accessibility is making sure that all content is perceivable. This means that text, images, and multimedia should be understandable to users with different sensory abilities. For users with visual impairments, websites should provide alternative text (alt text) for images, which can be read by screen readers. Additionally, videos should have captions or transcripts available for users who are deaf or hard of hearing. For those with cognitive impairments, content should be presented clearly and concisely, avoiding complex jargon and using simple language wherever possible.

Another important aspect of accessibility is operability, which ensures that users can interact with the web application through different input methods. This includes providing keyboard navigation for those who cannot use a mouse or touchscreen. All interactive elements, such as buttons, forms, and links, should be focusable and accessible via the keyboard. Developers should also make sure that the website can be operated with assistive technologies like voice control or switches, offering users alternative ways to navigate the site.

Web applications should also be designed with flexibility in mind, allowing users to customize the interface based on their needs. For example, users with low vision may need to adjust the font size or contrast of the content. A flexible layout that can be resized without losing functionality is essential to accommodate different devices and user preferences. Ensuring that your website is responsive and adaptable across various screen sizes can help improve accessibility for users with different devices, including smartphones and tablets.

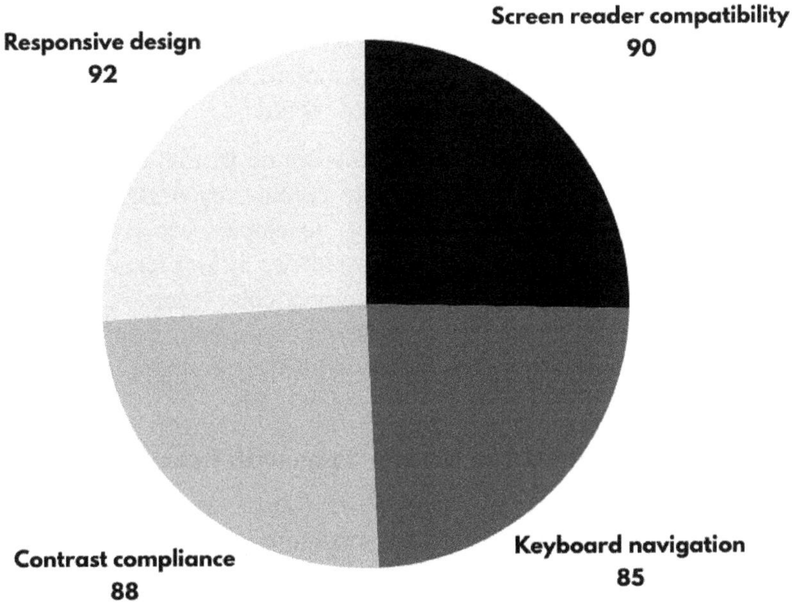

Figure 8.2 Evaluation of accessibility in web applications

The concept of robust design focuses on creating websites that work across a variety of browsers, devices, and assistive technologies. This means adhering to web standards and following best practices when writing HTML, CSS, and JavaScript. By ensuring that a website is compatible with a wide range of technologies, developers can ensure that users with disabilities can access content no matter what tools or devices they are using. Additionally, it is important to test the website for accessibility using automated tools, as well as manual testing with real users, to identify any issues that may affect users with disabilities.

Color contrast is another critical element in web accessibility. People with color blindness or low vision may struggle to read content if there is insufficient contrast between text and background colors. To make sure that content is easily readable, developers should follow the Web Content Accessibility Guidelines (WCAG) for color contrast ratios and choose color combinations that provide enough contrast for all users.

One of the key guidelines for web accessibility is ensuring that web applications can be used without relying on a mouse or other pointing device. This means that all functionality should be accessible via the keyboard alone, including navigation, form submission, and interactions with dynamic content. Focus management is also critical to ensure that users can follow the flow of the page when navigating with a keyboard or assistive device.

Accessibility should also be considered in the design of forms. Forms are one of the most common interactive elements on websites, but they can be difficult to use for individuals with motor impairments or cognitive disabilities. To improve form accessibility, developers should ensure that each form field is properly labeled with clear instructions and provide error messages that are easy to understand. Input fields should also be accessible via the keyboard, and users should be able to submit forms without relying on mouse clicks.

Finally, web developers should be mindful of the impact of dynamic content on accessibility. Websites that use JavaScript to dynamically update content should ensure that changes are announced to screen readers and other assistive technologies. Using ARIA (Accessible Rich Internet Applications) roles and properties, developers can inform users about changes to the page and ensure that the content remains accessible as it updates. Additionally, developers should make sure that interactive elements such as modals, sliders, and pop-ups are properly managed to prevent users from getting stuck or disoriented.

Accessibility in web applications is essential to ensuring that all users, regardless of their abilities or disabilities, can access and interact with content. By designing websites that are perceivable, operable, understandable, and robust, developers can create a more inclusive web experience. Key strategies for improving accessibility include providing alternative text for images, ensuring keyboard navigability, optimizing color contrast, creating responsive designs, and adhering to web standards. By considering accessibility from the beginning of the development process and testing for accessibility regularly, developers can ensure that their web applications are usable by the broadest audience possible.

8.5 Building Cross-Platform Mobile Apps with React Native

Building cross-platform mobile applications with React Native has become a popular approach due to its efficiency and ability to support both iOS and Android platforms with a single codebase. React Native, a framework developed by Facebook, allows developers to write mobile apps using JavaScript and React, a popular library for building user interfaces. The key advantage of React Native is its ability to bridge the gap between web development and mobile development, allowing developers to leverage their existing skills while delivering high-performance, native-like mobile experiences.

The React Native framework uses native components, enabling it to offer performance that is closer to native applications compared to traditional hybrid apps built using web technologies. React Native allows developers to write the majority of the app using JavaScript while still interacting with native code for tasks requiring higher performance or device-specific functionality, such as accessing device hardware, a camera, or GPS.

One of the core features of React Native is the concept of reusable components, which allows developers to create UI components that can be reused across both iOS and Android applications. Components in React Native are written in JavaScript and can use React's declarative syntax. This modular approach not only speeds up the development process but also makes it easier to maintain the app. A large collection of pre-built components and libraries provided by the React Native community can further accelerate development.

React Native relies on native modules to interact with device features that are not available out-of-the-box, such as camera access, GPS, or Bluetooth. Native modules allow developers to write platform-specific code in Objective-C, Swift (for iOS), or Java (for Android) and expose that functionality to JavaScript, making it accessible from within the app. This means that while React Native allows developers to build a unified codebase, they still have the flexibility to incorporate native code where necessary.

Another key aspect of React Native is its live reloading and hot reloading capabilities. Live reloading reloads the entire app after changes are made, while hot reloading only updates the components that have been modified without losing the app's state. These features significantly improve the development workflow, enabling faster iteration and testing of changes. Developers can immediately see the impact of their changes on the mobile device or emulator, which streamlines debugging and the development process.

Cross-platform development with React Native also ensures that code is shared across platforms, which leads to cost savings and reduced development time. This is because developers don't have to write separate code for iOS and Android. React Native uses platform-specific components and APIs, allowing for customized behavior for each platform while still sharing the majority of the code. For instance, while the user interface might look slightly different on iOS and Android due to platform-specific design guidelines, the underlying business logic remains consistent.

The React Native ecosystem offers a range of libraries and tools that support a wide variety of features required in mobile development. These include libraries for navigation (such as React Navigation), state management (such as Redux or Context API), and managing app lifecycle events. Integration with third-party services, APIs, and push notifications is also straightforward with available libraries and modules.

React Native offers an efficient and powerful way to build cross-platform mobile applications with a single codebase. By using JavaScript and React, developers can build high-performance, native-like apps for both iOS and Android. React Native's reusable components, live reloading, and vast ecosystem of libraries and tools make it an excellent choice for mobile app development. However, developers need to consider performance optimization, testing, and cross-device compatibility to ensure that their applications are fully functional and optimized for all users.

8.6 Emerging Trends in Web Technologies

Emerging trends in web technologies are constantly shaping how we interact with the web, driving new innovations and improving the overall web experience for both users and developers. As the internet evolves, several key trends are gaining momentum, each offering unique opportunities for enhancing web development and user engagement.

One of the most significant emerging trends is the rise of Progressive Web Applications (PWAs). PWAs combine the best features of web and mobile apps, offering a native-like experience directly in the browser. They are fast, reliable, and can work offline or in low-network conditions. PWAs are designed to load quickly, even with poor network connectivity, and they provide features like push notifications, background syncing, and home screen installation without the need for an app store. This approach reduces the cost and complexity of developing separate apps for different platforms while delivering a high-quality user experience.

Another key trend is WebAssembly (Wasm), a binary instruction format designed for safe, fast, and portable execution on the web. WebAssembly enables developers to run code written in languages like C, C++, and Rust directly in the browser, providing performance close to that of native applications. This is particularly useful for computationally intensive tasks like gaming, 3D rendering, and scientific simulations. With WebAssembly, developers can leverage existing libraries and write performance-critical code in languages other than JavaScript, expanding the possibilities of what can be achieved on the web.

The shift towards serverless architectures is also transforming web development. Serverless computing abstracts away the need for developers to manage server infrastructure, allowing them to focus on writing code while the cloud provider takes care of scaling and resource allocation. This architecture can lead to significant cost savings and improved scalability, as resources are only allocated when needed. Serverless functions are highly flexible, enabling developers to build microservices and APIs that can scale independently based on demand. Serverless technologies like AWS Lambda and Azure Functions are gaining popularity for building lightweight, event-driven applications.

Single-page applications (SPAs) continue to gain traction as developers seek to build faster, more responsive web applications. SPAs load a single HTML page and dynamically update content as the user interacts with the application, reducing the need for full-page reloads. This results in faster load times and a smoother user experience. Popular frameworks like React, Angular, and Vue.js are commonly used to build SPAs, and with advances in JavaScript engines and tools, SPAs have become more efficient and scalable. SPAs are particularly well-suited for applications with complex user interfaces and frequent interactions, such as social media platforms, e-commerce sites, and dashboards.

Artificial Intelligence (AI) and machine learning (ML) are rapidly being integrated into web applications, offering more personalized and intelligent user experiences. AI-powered chatbots, voice assistants, and recommendation systems are becoming commonplace on websites and e-commerce platforms, enhancing customer support and driving user engagement. Machine learning algorithms can analyze user behavior and preferences, allowing websites to offer tailored content and product recommendations. AI is also being used for automating tasks such as image recognition, language translation, and even content generation, making web apps more dynamic and capable.

Lastly, blockchain technology is beginning to influence web development, particularly in the areas of security and data transparency. Blockchain offers a decentralized way to store and transfer data, making it highly secure and resistant to fraud. Web applications that incorporate blockchain can offer secure transactions, identity verification, and data storage without relying on traditional centralized databases. While blockchain is still in its early stages, its potential for revolutionizing industries such as finance, supply chain, and healthcare is immense.

Web technologies continue to evolve rapidly, with emerging trends like Progressive Web Apps, WebAssembly, serverless architectures, and AI integration pushing the boundaries of what's possible. Developers are increasingly leveraging these technologies to build faster, more scalable, and more personalized web applications. Staying ahead of these trends allows developers to create cutting-edge web experiences that meet the growing demands of users while also improving performance, security, and scalability. As these technologies mature, they are likely to become integral to the future of web development.

9 Case Studies and Practical Applications

9.1 Building an E-Commerce Platform

Building an e-commerce platform requires a thorough understanding of both front-end and back-end technologies, user experience (UX) design, payment systems, and security protocols. It also involves addressing issues like scalability, product management, customer support, and integration with third-party services. With the increasing demand for online shopping, building a robust, scalable, and user-friendly e-commerce platform is crucial for businesses aiming to succeed in the digital marketplace.

The first step in building an e-commerce platform is determining the business model. Will it be a Business-to-Consumer (B2C) platform, a Business-to-Business (B2B) platform, or a marketplace that connects buyers and sellers? Understanding this will guide decisions on platform features and functionality. For example, B2C platforms may focus on delivering a seamless shopping experience for individual consumers, while B2B platforms may prioritize bulk ordering, pricing structures, and customer account management.

The front end of an e-commerce platform is critical for creating a user-friendly and visually appealing experience. A clean and intuitive layout, responsive design, and easy navigation are essential. Users should be able to easily browse products, filter by categories, and view detailed product pages with high-quality images, descriptions, and specifications. The checkout process should be simple and fast, minimizing friction points such as unnecessary form fields, hidden costs, or confusing navigation.

Figure 9.1 Building an e-Commerce platform

Back-end development for an e-commerce platform involves handling core business logic, managing user data, processing orders, and maintaining an inventory system. A powerful content management system (CMS) or e-commerce framework is required to handle product listings, customer accounts, inventory management, and order fulfillment. A well-structured database is essential for storing product details, customer information, and transaction history securely. The back-end should also integrate with payment gateways, ensuring smooth, secure transactions for customers.

A major component of any e-commerce platform is the payment system. E-commerce platforms need to integrate with secure, reliable payment gateways like PayPal, Stripe, or Square to process payments from various credit cards and digital wallets. It's important to ensure that transactions are encrypted and that sensitive customer data is handled securely to prevent fraud and unauthorized access. Offering multiple payment options, including installment plans or buy-now-pay-later services, can improve the customer experience and increase conversion rates.

One of the most important aspects of building an e-commerce platform is ensuring that it is secure. E-commerce websites are frequent targets for cyberattacks, so it's essential to implement security best practices. This includes SSL encryption for secure data transmission, two-factor authentication (2FA) for user accounts, and compliance with regulations such as the Payment Card Industry Data Security Standard (PCI DSS). Regular security audits and updates to the platform's software and infrastructure are essential to maintain a secure environment for customers.

Inventory management is another critical element of building an e-commerce platform. Inventory tracking systems ensure that products are in stock and available for order. These systems need to be integrated with the back-end to automatically update product availability as orders are placed. Additionally, e-commerce platforms should support the functionality to manage product variants, such as size, color, and quantity. This ensures that customers can easily select and purchase the right products without encountering issues related to stock levels or product availability.

For an e-commerce platform to be successful, it must provide a personalized shopping experience. This can be achieved by leveraging customer data to recommend products based on past purchases, browsing behavior, or demographic information. Personalization can increase engagement and conversion rates by making the shopping experience more relevant to individual users. Machine learning and artificial intelligence (AI) can be used to analyze customer behavior and automate product recommendations, promotions, and targeted content.

Lastly, integrating with third-party tools and services can enhance the functionality of the e-commerce platform. For example, email marketing tools can automate promotional campaigns, while analytics tools can provide insights into customer behavior and sales performance. Integration with CRM (Customer Relationship Management) systems helps businesses maintain detailed customer profiles and improve customer service. Additionally, social media integration allows users to share products and promotions, helping to increase visibility and attract new customers.

Building a successful e-commerce platform requires careful planning, efficient development, and attention to user experience, security, and scalability. A seamless front-end design, a robust back-end system, secure payment processing, and reliable inventory management are essential for ensuring a smooth and engaging shopping experience. By incorporating features like personalization, easy order fulfillment, and integration with third-party services, businesses can create a competitive online presence and increase their chances of success in the rapidly evolving e-commerce industry.

9.2 Developing a Real-Time Chat Application

Developing a real-time chat application involves several key elements to ensure that messages are transmitted and received instantly, offering a seamless experience for users. Whether it's for customer support, social interaction, or team collaboration, real-time chat applications are becoming increasingly essential across various platforms. The development of such an app combines front-end and back-end technologies, real-time communication protocols, user authentication, and data security.

The first consideration when building a real-time chat application is the communication protocol. WebSockets have become the standard for real-time communication on the web because they allow full-duplex communication channels over a single, long-lived connection between the client and server. Unlike traditional HTTP requests, where the client must repeatedly poll the server for updates, WebSockets enable the server to push updates to the client as soon as new data is available. This makes WebSockets an ideal choice for real-time applications like chat systems, where low-latency communication is essential.

On the back end, developers need to build the infrastructure that handles user connections, message storage, and the delivery of messages between users. A Node.js server is often used for real-time applications due to its non-blocking, event-driven nature, which allows it to handle multiple concurrent connections efficiently. Frameworks like Socket.io are commonly used in combination with Node.js for real-time communication, as they simplify the implementation of WebSockets and provide features such as reconnection, event handling, and broadcasting messages to multiple clients simultaneously.

User authentication is a crucial component of any chat application. It's essential to ensure that users can securely log in and that messages are only accessible to authorized individuals. There are various methods for authentication, such as using JWT (JSON Web Tokens), which is a secure way to transmit information between a client and a server. When a user logs in, the server generates a token that identifies the user, which is then sent to the client and used in subsequent requests. This allows for a secure, stateless way to verify users without having to store sensitive session data on the server.

In addition to authentication, user management features like profile creation, user status (online/offline), and the ability to add contacts or friends are essential for an interactive chat application. The front end must provide interfaces for users to sign up, log in, and manage their account settings. Additionally, status indicators, such as "typing..." or "last seen" timestamps, improve the user experience by providing real-time updates about the activity of other users in the chat.

For message delivery and storage, a messaging queue system, or a database designed for real-time data, is necessary. Many chat applications use NoSQL databases like MongoDB because of their ability to store unstructured data, handle rapid updates, and scale horizontally. The database stores messages, user information, and metadata, such as message timestamps or read/unread status. A messaging system needs to support storing chat history, retrieving past conversations quickly, and ensuring that messages are delivered reliably.

Lastly, performance optimization is key to providing a smooth and responsive user experience. The app should be optimized to handle large volumes of data with minimal delay. Techniques like lazy loading for messages, data compression for images and files, and efficient indexing in databases can help improve the performance of the chat application.

Building a real-time chat application requires integrating various technologies and practices to ensure a responsive, secure, and scalable platform. By utilizing WebSockets for real-time communication, implementing secure authentication, and focusing on performance and scalability, developers can create an engaging and efficient chat app. Features like user profiles, message storage, notifications, and rich media support help create a feature-rich and interactive experience for users, making the chat application an essential tool for modern communication.

9.3 Creating a Blogging Platform with CMS Features

Creating a blogging platform with content management system (CMS) features involves building a flexible and scalable application that allows users to create, manage, and publish blog posts with ease. A well-designed blogging platform should enable content creators to easily organize their work while providing features for customization, user engagement, and SEO optimization. The development process involves choosing the right technologies, designing an intuitive user interface, and integrating essential features like post management, media handling, and comment systems.

The back end of the blogging platform is responsible for managing data storage, user authentication, and content management. A CMS backend is typically built with a robust server-side framework such as Node.js, Django, Ruby on Rails, or Laravel. These frameworks allow for the creation of a scalable and maintainable application by handling data processing, server routing, and API creation. The platform's database, usually SQL (like PostgreSQL or MySQL) or NoSQL (like MongoDB), stores blog posts, user information, comments, and metadata. The database design should account for the structure of blog posts, categories, tags, user roles, and permissions.

For user authentication and management, developers often integrate OAuth or JWT for secure logins, allowing users to create accounts, sign in, and manage their profiles. Content creators should be able to create, edit, and delete posts, while admins may have additional privileges to moderate content and manage user roles. This can be achieved through role-based access control (RBAC), which allows for different levels of access and functionality based on user permissions.

The front end of a blogging platform is where the user experience takes center stage. It is essential to build a responsive, clean, and easy-to-navigate interface that allows users to quickly browse content and interact with posts. React, Vue.js, or Angular are commonly used JavaScript frameworks for creating dynamic, single-page applications (SPAs) that provide a smooth experience for users. A CMS-enabled platform allows users to view posts, search for content, and filter by categories, tags, or author. The front end should also include options for users to like or comment on posts, share them on social media, and subscribe to notifications for new content.

For content management, the CMS should enable easy creation and editing of blog posts, allowing users to format text, insert images or videos, and embed links. A rich text editor (like TinyMCE or Quill) provides an intuitive interface for writing and formatting posts, allowing for a WYSIWYG (What You See Is What You Get) experience. Posts should be categorized by topics or tags and organized in a way that makes it easy for users to find related content. For larger platforms, a multi-author system should be implemented, with features to manage posts from different authors and assign them to specific categories or topics.

To ensure a responsive design, the front end should be optimized for both desktop and mobile devices. Given the growing usage of mobile devices for reading blogs, it's crucial that the platform's design adjusts to different screen sizes, offering a smooth browsing experience. CSS frameworks like Bootstrap or Tailwind CSS are commonly used to speed up the development of responsive layouts.

Lastly, a blogging platform should be designed with security in mind. User data should be encrypted, and passwords should be securely hashed. The platform should be resistant to common web vulnerabilities, such as SQL injection, Cross-Site Scripting (XSS), and Cross-Site Request Forgery (CSRF). Regular security audits and software updates are essential for maintaining the integrity of the platform.

Building a blogging platform with CMS features requires careful planning and the integration of several key components, including user authentication, content management, media handling, SEO optimization, and user engagement tools. A clean, responsive front-end design, coupled with a powerful and scalable back-end, ensures that both content creators and readers have a seamless experience. Security, performance, and scalability considerations are crucial for building a reliable platform that can grow with its user base. By implementing these features and best practices, developers can create a dynamic and engaging blogging platform that supports content creators and fosters a thriving online community.

9.4 Scaling an application to Handle High Traffic

Scaling an application to handle high traffic involves improving its ability to manage increased demand, maintain performance, and ensure a smooth user experience even during peak usage periods. This is essential for applications that experience fluctuating or rapid growth in user base, such as e-commerce sites, social media platforms, or content-heavy websites. Effective scaling addresses various factors, including infrastructure, architecture, performance optimization, and

Table 9.1 Scaling strategies for handling high traffic applications

Scaling Technique	Description	Example
Load Balancing	Distributes traffic across multiple servers	Nginx, AWS ELB
Horizontal Scaling	Adds more servers to handle increased load	Adding more instances in Kubernetes
Vertical Scaling	Increases server resources (CPU, RAM, storage)	Upgrading to a higher-tier server
Caching	Stores frequently accessed data for faster retrieval	Redis, Memcached
Database Optimization	Improves query efficiency and data indexing	Using database indexing, read replicas

load distribution. By following best practices and leveraging modern tools and techniques, developers can create systems that scale efficiently and reliably.

The first step in scaling an application is ensuring that the architecture is designed to be scalable from the outset. A monolithic architecture, where all parts of the application are tightly integrated, can become a bottleneck as the user base grows. In contrast, a microservices architecture breaks down the application into smaller, independent services that can be scaled individually. This modular approach allows teams to scale different parts of the application as needed, depending on the specific demands of the service, whether it's user authentication, database access, or messaging.

One of the most critical aspects of scaling is load balancing, which helps distribute traffic evenly across servers to avoid overloading any single server. Load balancers can be deployed in various ways, including hardware-based or software-based solutions. Cloud services like AWS, Azure, and Google Cloud offer load balancing as part of their infrastructure, which allows for easy horizontal scaling of servers. The load balancer monitors the health of each server and routes requests to healthy instances, ensuring high availability and fault tolerance.

Horizontal scaling is a common approach to scaling an application. It involves adding more servers or instances to distribute the load rather than increasing the capacity of a single server (which is known as vertical scaling). Horizontal scaling is more cost-effective and resilient because it reduces the risk of a single point of failure. For web applications, cloud services allow automatic scaling of server instances based on traffic demands, meaning the application can handle spikes in traffic without manual intervention. Horizontal scaling also requires configuring services to be stateless so that any server can handle any request.

For data management, it's essential to implement database scaling techniques. Traditional databases can become a bottleneck under high traffic, especially when multiple users need to access and write data simultaneously. Sharding involves distributing data across multiple database servers or clusters to balance the load. This approach splits large datasets into smaller, more manageable pieces, making it easier to scale horizontally. Read replicas can also be employed to offload read-heavy database operations to separate servers, thus improving read performance. Additionally, NoSQL databases like MongoDB or Cassandra are often used for applications that require high write throughput and can benefit from distributed databases.

Another important aspect of scaling is caching. Caching stores frequently accessed data in memory to reduce the load on databases and improve response times. By serving cached data, the application can respond faster to requests, reducing the time spent querying the database. Popular caching solutions include Redis and Memcached, which store data in memory and provide rapid access. Caching can be implemented at various levels of the application, such as API responses, database queries, and even static assets like images and stylesheets. Implementing a content delivery network (CDN) to cache and deliver static content across geographically distributed servers can further optimize load times.

Asynchronous processing is another technique used to improve scalability. Not all tasks in an application need to be processed in real time. Tasks such as sending emails, processing images, or handling long-running computations can be offloaded to background workers or task queues. This ensures that the main application can remain responsive to user requests while heavy operations are handled asynchronously. Tools like RabbitMQ, Amazon SQS, or Celery enable developers to create task queues, allowing time-consuming operations to be processed in the background without impacting the overall performance of the application.

Scaling an application to handle high traffic requires a multi-faceted approach involving architecture design, load balancing, horizontal scaling, database management, caching, asynchronous processing, and monitoring. Leveraging cloud services and modern development practices like auto-scaling, disaster recovery, and continuous delivery ensures that an application can scale effectively while maintaining performance and reliability. By addressing these challenges, businesses can ensure that their applications are capable of handling high traffic and providing a smooth user experience, even under the most demanding conditions.

9.5 Cloud-Based Image and Video Hosting

Cloud-based image and video hosting has become an essential solution for businesses and developers looking to manage, store, and deliver high-quality media content efficiently. Traditional hosting solutions often struggle to meet the demands of media-heavy applications, particularly when dealing with large file sizes, high traffic, and the need for fast, reliable delivery. Cloud-based hosting, provided by services like Amazon S3, Google Cloud Storage, and Azure Blob Storage, addresses these challenges by offering scalable, secure, and highly available infrastructure designed specifically for handling media files.

One of the primary advantages of cloud-based hosting is scalability. Traditional on-premises servers can become overwhelmed as media files grow in size or number, especially if they are subject to fluctuating demand. Cloud providers offer auto-scaling capabilities, which means that resources can be dynamically allocated to handle sudden spikes in traffic without manual intervention. This scalability ensures that the application remains responsive and can deliver content efficiently, even during peak times.

Cost-effectiveness is another key benefit of cloud-based hosting. Rather than investing in physical infrastructure, cloud hosting operates on a pay-as-you-go model. This means businesses only pay for the storage and bandwidth they use, allowing for significant cost savings. Additionally, cloud providers offer different tiers of storage, allowing users to choose the level of performance they need based on the nature of their media. For example, a low-resolution image might not require the same storage capacity or bandwidth as a high-definition video, and the cloud solution can scale accordingly.

Cloud-based platforms also provide global content delivery via Content Delivery Networks (CDNs). CDNs store cached copies of media files on servers located in various regions around the world. This ensures that users can access media content from a server geographically closer to them, reducing latency and improving load times. For example, when a user in Europe accesses a video hosted in the U.S., a CDN can serve the video from a European server, ensuring a faster and smoother viewing experience.

Another benefit of cloud hosting is security. Cloud providers invest heavily in security measures such as encryption, access controls, and data redundancy to protect media files. Files stored in the cloud can be encrypted both at rest (when stored) and in transit (when being accessed or transferred), providing a high level of data protection. Additionally, cloud services offer access management tools, which allow administrators to control who can view, upload, or modify media files, ensuring that only authorized users have access.

Managing large media libraries can be a challenge, but cloud hosting services provide robust media management tools to make this task easier. Many cloud providers offer APIs and management consoles that allow users to upload, organize, and search for images and videos. Media can be categorized with metadata, tagged with keywords, and indexed for easy retrieval.

Some cloud platforms also offer features like image optimization and automatic transcoding, which can adjust the resolution, format, or size of videos and images based on the end user's device or network speed.

In addition to basic storage and delivery, many cloud providers offer advanced features such as image processing and video transcoding. Cloud services can automatically resize, crop, or apply filters to images, enabling dynamic content delivery based on the user's preferences or device specifications. Similarly, video transcoding allows for the conversion of videos into different formats and resolutions to support various devices, from smartphones to high-definition televisions, ensuring that content is accessible across all platforms.

Cloud-based hosting also integrates seamlessly with other cloud-based services, such as databases, machine learning tools, and analytics platforms. This integration allows for the creation of more sophisticated applications, where media files can be processed, analyzed, or tagged automatically. For example, image recognition models can automatically tag photos with relevant keywords, or machine learning algorithms can analyze video content to generate metadata for search and categorization.

Finally, integration with third-party applications is a crucial aspect of cloud-based hosting. Many platforms offer pre-built integrations with popular CMS (Content Management Systems), marketing platforms, and other web applications, making it easy to incorporate media hosting into existing workflows. For example, developers can integrate cloud-hosted media into a website, mobile app, or social media platform with ease, ensuring seamless content delivery across multiple channels.

Cloud-based image and video hosting provides a scalable, cost-effective, and secure solution for managing and delivering media content. By leveraging cloud services, businesses can offer fast, reliable, and global access to images and videos, all while optimizing performance, ensuring data security, and benefiting from advanced media management and processing capabilities. Whether it's a small blog or a large-scale video streaming platform, cloud hosting enables developers to focus on building great user experiences without worrying about the underlying infrastructure.

10 Conclusion and Future Outlook

10.1 Recap of Key Takeaways

Cloud-Based Hosting Benefits: Cloud-based image and video hosting provides scalability, security, and cost-effectiveness. It allows for dynamic scaling based on traffic demands, ensuring smooth performance during peak usage.

Global Content Delivery: Using Content Delivery Networks (CDNs) helps to reduce latency by caching media at servers located around the world, ensuring faster load times and a better user experience, especially for global users.

Security and Data Protection: Cloud providers implement robust security measures like encryption, access controls, and redundancy to protect media files from unauthorized access and data loss.

Advanced Media Management: Cloud hosting services offer tools for managing large media libraries, including metadata organization, search functionality, and optimization features such as image resizing and video transcoding.

Integration and Flexibility: Cloud hosting integrates seamlessly with other cloud-based services like databases, machine learning, and analytics platforms, providing enhanced capabilities for media processing and performance optimization.

Cost Efficiency: Cloud hosting uses a pay-as-you-go model, reducing upfront infrastructure costs and allowing businesses to only pay for the resources they actually use, making it an affordable solution for managing media content.

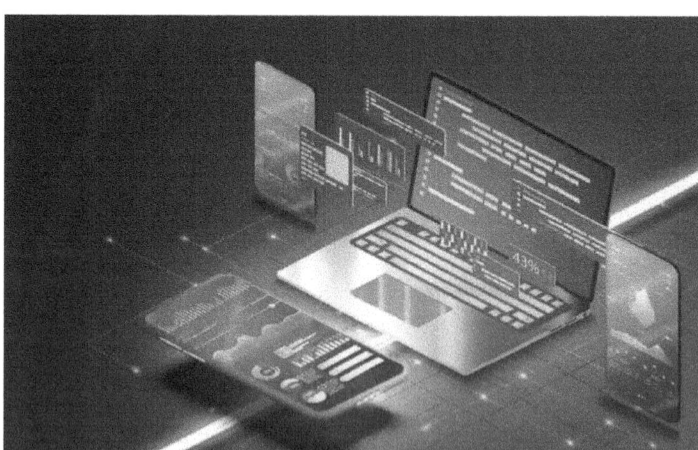

Figure 10.1 Preparing for future trends in web development

Performance Optimization: Techniques like caching, file compression, and adaptive streaming technologies ensure that media is delivered quickly and efficiently, even under varying network conditions.

Backup and Disaster Recovery: Cloud solutions offer redundancy and disaster recovery features, ensuring that media files are safe and easily recoverable in case of system failures or data loss.

Analytics and Reporting: Cloud platforms provide valuable insights into media file usage, allowing businesses to track performance, user engagement, and optimize their content delivery strategies.

Third-Party Integration: Cloud-based hosting can be easily integrated with other applications such as content management systems and marketing tools, enabling streamlined workflows and enhanced media management.

10.2 Preparing for Future Trends in Web Development

Preparing for future trends in web development involves staying ahead of emerging technologies, adopting best practices, and continuously adapting to changing user expectations and business needs. The web development landscape is constantly evolving, with new tools, frameworks, and methodologies shaping the way applications are built, deployed, and experienced. By anticipating and preparing for these trends, developers can ensure that they are ready to deliver cutting-edge solutions while remaining competitive in a fast-paced environment.

One of the most significant trends shaping the future of web development is the continued rise of progressive web applications (PWAs). PWAs combine the best features of web and mobile apps, offering fast loading times, offline capabilities, and app-like experiences without the need for installation from an app store. With the increasing reliance on mobile devices, PWAs are becoming a preferred solution for businesses looking to provide a seamless, engaging user experience across all devices.

Another key trend is the growing importance of serverless architecture. Serverless computing allows developers to focus on writing code without worrying about managing the underlying infrastructure. By leveraging cloud platforms and Functions-as-a-Service (FaaS), developers can build highly scalable, cost-efficient applications that automatically scale based on traffic, without the need for provisioning or maintaining servers. This trend is especially useful for small to medium-sized businesses looking to reduce infrastructure costs while maintaining high performance.

Single-page applications (SPAs) continue to dominate as the preferred architecture for modern web applications. SPAs deliver faster and smoother user experiences by loading content dynamically without refreshing the entire page. This is achieved through frameworks like React, Vue.js, and Angular, which provide the necessary tools for building dynamic, responsive web applications. SPAs are particularly popular in content-heavy websites, dashboards, and social media platforms, where real-time updates and quick transitions are crucial.

The integration of artificial intelligence (AI) and machine learning (ML) is becoming a major trend in web development. AI-powered tools and algorithms are enabling personalized experiences, smart chatbots, recommendation engines, and enhanced user interfaces. By using AI and ML in web applications, businesses can automate tasks, gain insights from data, and offer more tailored experiences to users. As AI technologies continue to improve, developers will need to incorporate these capabilities into their applications to stay competitive.

Another trend that is expected to grow in prominence is Web 3.0 and blockchain technology. Web 3.0 represents the next evolution of the internet, focusing on decentralization, privacy, and user empowerment. Blockchain is at the core of Web 3.0, offering secure, transparent ways to store and share data without relying on centralized authorities. In the future, web developers will need to understand how to integrate blockchain technology into their applications for secure transactions, identity management, and data integrity.

The rise of low-code/no-code development platforms is also a trend that is reshaping web development. These platforms allow users with little or no coding experience to build web applications through intuitive drag-and-drop interfaces and pre-built templates. While these tools are not a replacement for traditional developers, they enable rapid prototyping, reduce development costs, and allow non-technical stakeholders to participate in the development process.

Web accessibility continues to be a critical focus in the web development community. As regulations like the Americans with Disabilities Act (ADA) and the European Union's Web Accessibility Directive become more stringent, developers must ensure that their applications are usable by people with disabilities. This involves adhering to accessibility standards like WCAG (Web Content Accessibility Guidelines) and using semantic HTML, ARIA (Accessible Rich Internet Applications) attributes, and other tools to create inclusive web experiences.

5G technology is set to have a profound impact on web development by enabling faster internet speeds, lower latency, and more reliable connections. With 5G, developers will be able to create applications that require real-time interactions, such as augmented reality (AR) and virtual reality (VR) experiences. The increase in bandwidth and decrease in latency will allow for more immersive and data-heavy applications that were previously not feasible on mobile devices.

As privacy concerns continue to grow, data protection and privacy regulations will remain a major focus. With stricter laws like the General Data Protection Regulation (GDPR) in the European Union and the California Consumer Privacy Act (CCPA) in the U.S., developers will need to prioritize user consent, data encryption, and transparency in how personal data is collected, stored, and used. Future web applications must be designed to protect user privacy while complying with evolving regulations.

Finally, cloud computing and containerization will continue to play a major role in the future of web development. Cloud-based infrastructure enables scalable, flexible hosting solutions that can handle fluctuating demand without the need for on-premises hardware. Containers, such as Docker, provide a lightweight and portable way to deploy applications, ensuring consistency across different environments. As businesses increasingly move to the cloud, web developers will need to adopt cloud-native architectures and container orchestration tools like Kubernetes to build modern, scalable applications.

The future of web development is shaped by a range of emerging technologies and trends that prioritize performance, scalability, security, and user experience. By staying informed about these developments and incorporating them into their workflows, developers can position themselves for success in an ever-evolving digital landscape. As new tools and platforms continue to emerge, web developers will need to be adaptable and continuously learn to remain at the forefront of innovation.

10.3 Resources for Continued Learning

Continued learning is essential for web developers who want to stay up-to-date with the rapidly evolving landscape of web technologies. Fortunately, there are a wealth of resources available to help developers keep their skills sharp and stay informed about the latest trends and best practices. Below are some valuable resources for continued learning in web development:

10.3.1 Online Courses and Tutorials

freeCodeCamp: A popular free resource offering interactive courses on web development, including HTML, CSS, JavaScript, and advanced topics like Node.js, React, and databases.

Udemy: An online platform offering a wide range of affordable courses on web development, from beginner to advanced levels. Courses on specific frameworks, libraries, and technologies like React, Angular, Vue.js, and Node.js are particularly useful.

Codecademy: An interactive learning platform with hands-on coding exercises and projects. Codecademy offers paths for front-end and back-end development, including JavaScript, HTML, CSS, and full-stack development.

Coursera: It offers courses from universities and institutions on web development, including specializations in front-end and back-end development, web design, and cloud technologies.

Pluralsight: A subscription-based platform that provides in-depth tutorials on a wide variety of web development topics, including JavaScript, cloud computing, and security.

10.3.2 Documentation and Official Guides

MDN Web Docs (Mozilla Developer Network): The go-to resource for web developers, with comprehensive documentation on HTML, CSS, JavaScript, APIs, and web standards. It's an authoritative guide for web development best practices.

React Documentation: The official React documentation provides an in-depth look at how to build user interfaces with React, including tutorials and concepts like hooks, state management, and component life cycles.

Vue.js Documentation: Vue's official docs provide tutorials, API references, and examples for building applications with Vue.js, a progressive JavaScript framework.

Angular Documentation: The official Angular documentation offers detailed explanations of Angular concepts, tutorials, and guides on using Angular for building dynamic web applications.

Node.js Documentation: The official Node.js documentation provides everything from installation guides to API references, useful for developers building server-side applications.

10.3.3 Books and E-books

"You Don't Know JS" (Kyle Simpson): A series of books that dive deep into JavaScript, ideal for developers who want to master JavaScript and understand its inner workings.

"JavaScript: The Good Parts" (Douglas Crockford): A concise guide that focuses on the most important and effective features of JavaScript.

"Eloquent JavaScript" (Marijn Haverbeke): A well-regarded book that covers JavaScript fundamentals and advanced topics, with exercises and projects to practice.

"Designing Data-Intensive Applications" (Martin Kleppmann): A great resource for developers interested in learning about databases, distributed systems, and how to build scalable, resilient web applications.

"Learning React" (Alex Banks & Eve Porcello): A hands-on book that helps developers learn React.js by building real-world applications.

10.3.4 Podcasts and YouTube Channels

JavaScript Jabber: A podcast that covers all things JavaScript, including interviews with developers and discussions on frameworks, libraries, and development practices.

The Changelog: A podcast focused on open-source software and development trends. It features interviews with prominent developers, offering insights into the latest tools and technologies.

Frontend Masters YouTube Channel: Offers high-quality web development content, including tutorials on JavaScript, React, Vue.js, CSS, and web performance optimization.

The Net Ninja: A YouTube channel that provides comprehensive tutorials on web development topics, including front-end frameworks, Node.js, and full-stack development.

Traversy Media: Another popular YouTube channel for web developers, featuring tutorials on JavaScript, React, Node.js, and various web development tools.

10.3.5 Communities and Forums

Stack Overflow: A Q&A platform where developers can ask questions, share knowledge, and find solutions to common programming problems.

GitHub: A platform for version control and collaboration. Developers can contribute to open-source projects, explore other developers' code, and learn from real-world applications.

Dev.to: A community of developers who share articles, tutorials, and insights into the latest trends in web development. It's a great place to engage with other developers and learn from each other.

Reddit (r/webdev, r/learnjavascript): Subreddits where developers discuss web development topics, share resources, and ask questions. It's a great place for discovering new tools and staying informed on trends.

Slack and Discord Communities: Many web development communities exist on Slack and Discord, where developers discuss topics, share knowledge, and help each other with coding issues in real time.

10.3.6 Experimentation and Open Source Projects

Building Projects: One of the best ways to learn is by doing. Work on personal projects, contribute to open-source repositories, or clone popular apps to gain hands-on experience.

GitHub Open Source: Explore popular open-source projects to learn from the code, contribute to development, and understand how large-scale applications are structured and maintained.

By utilizing these resources, developers can continue expanding their knowledge, keeping up with the latest trends, and improving their web development skills. Continuous learning is essential in the ever-changing field of web development, and these resources provide an excellent foundation for growth and success in the industry.

www.ingramcontent.com/pod-product-compliance
Ingram Content Group UK Ltd.
Pitfield, Milton Keynes, MK11 3LW, UK
UKHW061547190726
13845UKWH00030B/1062

9 788198 754356